Letters from the DHAMMA BROTHERS

Dhamma is a word in Pali, the language spoken by Gotama the Buddha (*Dharma* in Sanskrit). It means the Way, the Truth, the Buddha's teachings. The group of inmates who took the first Vipassana course together at Donaldson Correctional Facility call themselves "the Dhamma Brothers" in recognition of their shared experiences.

Letters from the
DHAMMA BROTHERS

Meditation Behind Bars

Jenny Phillips

Pariyatti Press

First Edition, Pariyatti Press, 2008.

ISBN-13 978-1-928706-31-1
12 11 10 09 08 07 5 4 3 2 1

Library of Congress Control Number: 2006938697

The publisher gratefully acknowledges Judith Fox Lee for substantive editing
and the many others who have helped bring this book to completion,
including LeRoy Allen and Andy Kukura for providing photographs, Ron
Cavanaugh for his help in obtaining photo releases and Candace Ohanessian
and Pamela Solarz for transcribing the letters.

Cover design based on *The Dhamma Brothers* film poster, courtesy Northern Lights
Productions.

Pariyatti Press
867 Larmon Road, Onalaska, WA 98570
www.pariyatti.org

Distributed to the trade by Independent Publishers Group

Dedicated to the Dhamma Brothers:

Ricky Alexander
Grady Bankhead
Torrence Barton
Troy Bridges
Michael Carpenter
Willie Carroll
Warren Cooke
Eli Crawford
Russell Cutts
Edward L. Daughtry
Charles Dobbins
Frederick W. Finch
Manson Fischer Jr.
James George
Benjamin Harvey
Charles Ice
Edward C. Johnson
John W. Johnson
Kenneth Jones
Leon Kennedy
David Lucas
Milton Lucas
Torsten Norris
O.B. Benjamin Oryang
Sheldon Padgett
Lataurus Peoples
Omar Rahman
Timothy Shreve
William Simmons
Stafford Simpson
Larry Singletary
Rick Smith
Calvin Steward
James L. Wayne
Marvin Wooden
Johnny Mack Young

CONTENTS

FOREWORD

Robert Coles

As I was turning the pages that follow, my mind got carried back to my work with troubled young people in Boston during the late 1950's—"juvenile delinquents" they were then called—some of them in serious trouble with the law and a few already jailed or on probation. I was also visiting prisons and talking with men kept under lock and key for serious crimes, ranging from robbery to assault and battery and even murder.

I would, of course, try to accomplish what my training in psychiatry and psychoanalysis had taught me to do: Listen long and hard and offer what thoughts came to my mind, observations, clarifications, interpretations. Often, as I went about such efforts, I had no great confidence that anything I had to offer would make any difference. These were troubled, hard men, and most of them had little trouble expressing their disdain for my ilk with a curt remark, a turning away of the head, a shrug of the shoulders. After a while I found myself echoing what no doubt frequently crossed their minds: how long until I'd be back on the outside, away from the prison where I was sitting at that moment. Similarly, several of those with whom I was trying to talk made no bones, through a grimace or an outright comment, of their wish to go back to their place of confinement rather than sit with me and reflect upon what had gotten them into their predicament.

One afternoon as I sat talking to a young man who had assaulted two individuals, broken into a home and stolen goods there, then badly injured a storekeeper who resisted his demand for money (and who later died of the robber's gunshot wound), I heard this: "What's your problem, mister doctor?" Then a bold and angry denunciation of me and my kind: "I've met a lot of you guys. You keep trying to get me to answer your questions. By now, I know you all—and where you're trying to go with me in tow. No way!" Then a spell of determined, stony silence, his head bowed—after which, a glare that would not let up. He had me stymied, to say the least, and of course, uptight if not frozen in silence as I contemplated what to say and how to get this "therapeutic session" going again.

Finally, the unnerving silence that had gripped both of us came to a merciful if troubling conclusion, at the behest of the one who sat across the table that separated us: "The only way I'll get rid of the trouble I'm in is to get rid of myself." Silence—as I pondered what to say. Then a shrewdly stunning remark that had my mind reeling: "I need to sit and think, and sit and think, until I get rid of my bad self and become a better guy. Throw out the junk, the bad side, and find the good inside, the one who can smile at the world and shake hands with it, not try to cuff it, kick it, bloody it up. I'll be in jail anyway but better cleaned up than stinking with lousy thoughts."

Silence, as I tried to grasp what I'd heard, then respond with some intelligence and tact. In a few seconds, as if my perplexity needed to be further adjusted: "Hey, my uncle fought in the Second World War; he landed in Iwo Jima, taking on the Japs. A lot of his buddies never made it out of that hellhole of an island. My uncle kept praying that he'd stay alive, and after the war was over, he got a job that landed him in India where he learned about Buddhism: You struggle to win yourself, for your bigger, better self. You stop yourself in your tracks. You say, 'Whoa! Enough of wasting time and energy, running around in circles!' After a while you're not going all over the place, you're sitting still, and you're turning into yourself. And the static outside, you hold your ears to keep it out, and the same goes for the sights meant to get you to go here, there, everywhere, and buy, buy, until you're broke."

A pause and then an account of his uncle's "Buddhist talk" which he had scorned until now: "I've got a lot of junk in me to face squarely, then toss out, but it'll be no easy job, I know." At that point I had little to say. I felt I was hearing plenty, enough for me to ponder with respect to myself, never mind regarding the young person sitting with me in the jail.

As I recall that clinical time, I realize how much we have to learn from others, from fellow human beings, be they "uncles," "patients," or "prisoners." We hand one another along, as Walker Percy tells us. As Buddhists have learned to know about themselves, we search for ourselves, attend ourselves, until we are there, having grasped, realized, and found ourselves, and so become able to join in with others, fellow seekers eager to affirm our shared humanity through inquiry and reflection and find release from a kind of blindness, deafness, thoughtlessness, and yes, imprisonment. Some of those we meet in the pages of this book have managed through their minds' patient, persistent, knowing introspective efforts to confront and then at last become decisively free within of the old, crushing weight of heedless impulse run harmfully rampant—brothers now in a shared, inwardly energetic thoughtfulness.

All of the above came to my mind as I turned page after page of this extraordinarily telling and inspiring book, its contents a witness to the human connection achieved. A psychologically knowing observer, Jenny Phillips manages to enable the far off, the imprisoned, to become the reader's informants and teachers so that a prison brotherhood can become a universal brother- and sisterhood and a narration becomes a spur to the reader's reflective life.

Robert Coles
Concord, Massachusetts
November 19, 2007

INTRODUCTION

Lucia Meijer

I came to know Vipassana while managing the North Rehabilitation Facility, a 291-bed adult detention facility in the King County, Washington, jail system with a focus on addictions treatment. Impressed by the Vipassana concept and its representatives, I agreed to accommodate an ongoing program of ten-day courses for inmates over five years. Even more surprisingly, I agreed to take a course myself. Vipassana became a regular fixture at NRF as it did in my personal life. Despite my absolute belief in the efficacy of this practice, after 30 years of working with and around "hard-core" addicts in and out of custody, I'm often skeptical of attempts at offender rehabilitation. I believe that the primary benefit of any rehabilitation effort lies not only in the potential impact on an offender but also in the civilizing influence it has on the rest of us. It's always preferable to be guided by pragmatic societal self-interest than by the fleeting satisfaction—and inevitable backlash—of outraged retribution.

These letters from Donaldson inmates reveal more than they say, more perhaps than the authors intended. They were not written without effort. For many who populate our jails and prisons, the written word can be a difficult tool to wield. Despite low literacy levels, inmates must often depend on written communications for many of their basic needs. I've seen inmates struggle to fill out simple (and not so simple) forms that can make the difference between whether or not they get medical attention, drug treatment, or a special visit with a family member. Communications outside of the institution are even more limited. Visits and phone calls are rushed and seldom private. So, undereducated inmates will spend hours laboring over a letter—trying to connect with fragmented, often traumatized family members, asking for forgiveness, for love, for money, for control, but nearly always asking. Inmates are experts in asking.

This chronic neediness is not only a result of incarceration, but often its precursor. Powerlessness traps us in eternal childhood. Unable to be self-sufficient, we become dependent, fearful, ashamed and resentful. Typical inmate behaviors include lying, boasting, blaming and manipulating. Over time, these ways of coping become deeply ingrained personality traits. Reality is buried under a mountain of denial and depersonalization. I've heard inmates talk about their crimes as if they weren't there when it happened; their addictions as a struggle between good and evil "forces" beyond their control; their victims as complicit in the crime. They often blame the victim, the cops, the courts, the "system"—anything to distance themselves from the unbearable reality of their own guilt, shame and regret.

As I read these letters, I see familiar personal disclosures, attempts at intimacy and self-enhancement, effusive expressions of love, appreciation and gratitude. I've seen this before: Men and women who have thrown everything and everyone into the fire of their own destructive impulses suddenly transformed into caring, attentive, insightful converts. As I said, I am a skeptic; I read their letters with a critical eye.

In these letters, however, there is something I haven't seen before. These inmates have unexpectedly begun to ask something more of themselves as well as from others. Often it is a new-found compassion toward fellow inmates, a motivation to participate constructively in a difficult environment, a desire to give, tolerance of harsh conditions and arbitrary rules, a willingness to face unbearable memories. Reading their letters, I don't see men magically transformed into new people. I see men facing who they really are. What is transformed is their ability to see—to have the courage and maturity to look into their own lives and minds.

When I talk about the impact Vipassana had on all of us at the jail, I am invariably asked about inmate outcomes. Everyone always wants to know what will happen now that eyes, minds and hearts have been opened. Are these inmates truly reformed? If given the chance, will they reoffend? Can they be trusted now? I can't answer these questions for the inmates who wrote these letters. I've been meditating in this tradition for almost ten years now—can I always be *completely* trusted? My own lapses are not criminal, but they are typical. All I can say is, what these inmates experienced and what it changed about them is real, and that gives me hope for all of us.

Lucia Meijer
Former Administrator, North Rehabilitation Facility
President, North American Vipassana Prison Trust

LETTERS FROM THE DHAMMA BROTHERS

JENNY PHILLIPS

INSIDE DONALDSON

Graduation

Twenty prison inmates sat in a semi-circle on plastic chairs in the prison's West Gymnasium. They had just completed a continuous ten-day retreat in which they had meditated in silence and stillness for over ten hours each day. On this day these men became the first inmates inside a United States maximum-security prison to complete such a rigorous program based on the 2,600-year-old teachings of the Buddha.

Now the prison warden and the director of treatment for the Alabama Department of Corrections sat in the audience to listen to the testimony of these men. Various prison treatment and security staff, as well as inmates invited from the prison population of 1,500, had gathered to hear what the men had to say about their personal experiences in this most unusual program. One by one, 20 men stepped to the front of the room, held the microphone, and described what they had been through. They ranged in age from their early twenties to their fifties.

Edward Johnson, a tall, thin man who had spent many years in a segregation cell, thanked the warden and the prison psychologist for believing that he could be a "better man." Their confidence in him had allowed him to survive "the long hours on the meditation cushion." As he spoke, he wept openly. Many of the other men began to weep. Next, Michael Carpenter, a slight young man, came to the microphone and spoke in hushed tones. "Twelve years ago I received life without parole. I thought that was my punishment. But I didn't realize that I could punish myself worse than the judge. During the past ten days I have seen how I have beat up on myself for many years for ending up in prison. But I feel like I am on a new path now and that I have learned what I need to know to go down this path." A young African American named Benjamin Harvey said, "This was a magnificent experience. But at first I wanted to leave. I didn't know I had so much anger, depression and hurt balled up inside. But the teachers told me, 'Don't run. Get to the root.' So I stayed and I worked, and by the eighth day all the garbage had come to the surface and I felt so much better."

As Warden Stephen Bullard listened to the testimony of the men, he was impressed by their open sincerity. He had wondered if they would "fake it 'til they make it" when he had first considered whether to hold the program in his prison. After all had spoken, he turned to them and praised them for their courage.

"People wonder why I choose to work in a prison. I don't want to beat people down. I want to improve this prison." In the prison world of strictly enforced hierarchy and control, Warden Bullard was reaching across the great divide between his office as jailer and keeper of the keys into the realm of the kept and the stigmatized. He now further narrowed the distance between himself and the inmates when he said, "I could easily be sitting in one of your chairs if things had turned out differently. I could still end up in one of your chairs—you never know. But now that this course has ended, I want you to go back into the prison and become agents of change. I am proud of this program and pleased that today we have become part of prison history."

How did this extraordinary program come to be? Prisoners in the deep South, inside a maximum-security prison, had spent ten days practicing an ancient, intensive meditation technique. This was certainly one of the most innovative treatment programs ever tried in a prison. It was carried out with a strong level of commitment and sacrifice in a state prison system struggling with severe overcrowding and an equally severe lack of resources and staff. To answer this question, it is necessary to look more thoroughly into the prison itself, to consider the harshness and hopelessness of daily life there as well as the recent appearance within the prison of countervailing forces for positive change.

The Journey Inside

W. E. Donaldson Correctional Facility is set in the Alabama countryside south of Birmingham, in the midst of thick woodland, red clay soil and tangled kudzu vines. Wrapped around it on three sides, coiled like a snake as it flows south to the Gulf Coast, is the Black Warrior River. Donaldson's inmates live behind high security towers and a double row of barbed and electrified razor wire fences. The wire, capable of delivering a lethal charge, gleams and glints in the sunlight with disarming beauty. This is a place for those who may never be released back into society, inmates with the

W. E. Donaldson Correctional Facility

longest stays and the highest levels of crime. Many are sentenced to life without parole, virtually condemning them to a lifetime behind prison walls. Many others have life sentences, some for nonviolent crimes based on the "three-strikes-you're-out" policy instituted during the 1990s. The prison houses a population of inmates on death row and has a mental health unit for those with severe mental illness. Referred to by its residents as the "House of Pain," Donaldson is the prison where the most unmanageable and intransigent of Alabama's inmates are sent.

Although a small trickle of inmates is released back into the outside world, there is a distinct atmosphere within these prison walls of a separate, contained society. Once inside, inmates are stripped of their "free-world" identity and possessions, and henceforth must live on the paucity of standard prison-issue goods. Except for phone calls and occasional visits, they must rebuild their lives inside the prison, associating mainly with other inmates and letting go of the outside world. They live lives of enforced simplicity and regimentation, a large number of people living in a small space on few resources.

I first visited Donaldson in the fall of 1999. Driving down the long, isolated road leading to the prison, there is a sense of having reached a border crossing into a foreign land. Suddenly the prison looms ahead, a long low structure dotted with control towers. At the front office there is a check and search and a walk through a metal detector. Next, a door is buzzed open allowing passage into a metal cage with a gate on either end, both of which are electronically controlled by an armed guard in a tower. The first gate must be closed before the second one opens at the other end. This is followed by a short passage through a no-man's-land, a grassy lawn sandwiched between the exterior and interior prison walls, that brings one inside the prison. After passing the administrative offices there is a final locked door. Once through this door, both the architectural and psychological landscapes change dramatically.

When one enters the building there is a distinct feeling of having left

Uniformity and movement

behind all that is familiar and taken for granted. The first person one meets inside is an inmate shining shoes at a stand. Wide corridors form a "V" stretching away from the stand to the east and west. Even though one is now "inside," there is a final metal gate which slowly slides open, traversing this corridor. As it slams shut, the visitor from the "free world" enters an alien place based on forced containment and control.

There is a stench of sweat and disinfectant and an aura of misery and suppressed violence. Painted in hues of brown, the corridors are long, dark and dank. In hot weather, steam and mist rise and drip from the walls, and the floors are slippery with moisture. Inmates in white pants and shirts, with *Alabama Department of Corrections* emblazoned on their backs, continually move up and down the corridors. Everyone stays to the right, systematically marching along like ants in a colony. They seem to be going somewhere, but their range is sharply demarcated by the prison's physical boundaries. The stereotypical image of prisons is of inmates neatly locked away in cells, of quiet halls traveled by officers with keys. But these inmates are out and about. Much of the traffic consists of a flow to and from the dining hall. Men are also moving to school programs and prison-based jobs. The din and movement, however, is that of controlled activity. Moving among the inmates are staff and unarmed corrections officers carrying night sticks and two-way radios.

All of the inmates are dressed in the stark, white, prison-issue clothing with black, stenciled lettering. Displayed prominently on the left front of each shirt is the identification number whose six digits become an inmate's primary identity. Similarly, each prisoner's address is essentially the location of a bed. Many live with another inmate or two in a small cell on a cell block. One inmate referred to this living situation as "living in a closet with a stranger." Some prefer living in such cells because of the relative privacy they offer. While there is no sense of ownership or property, there is some control over this small space constructed of concrete blocks and metal bars.

By contrast, others live in open dormitories of more than 100 beds separated by less than two feet of open space. This arrangement allows more freedom of movement and access to a large yard and track for exercising. But the trade-off is a total lack of privacy and control of personal space. A prisoner's home is reduced to a bunk and a locked box underneath containing his possessions. Most activities take place on or around this bunk. Life becomes reduced to its barest essentials. There is an open bathroom on one side of this room with a long, shared shower stall, an open urinal trough, and two or three toilets immediately next to each another. Men must sit side by side on these toilets, with no partition or screen for privacy. In this enormous room all activities are communal and open to public view. The noise and activity are pervasive and never-ending. Two television sets blast their programs. Ceiling lights are on all day and much of the night. The smell of crowded bodies saturates the atmosphere.

I decided to visit Donaldson because I had heard that several hundred inmates there had studied the Houses of Healing meditation program and were now meditating regularly. I am a licensed psychotherapist and have a doctorate in cultural anthropology. For several years I had been teaching the same meditation-based group therapy course to men in some Massachusetts prisons. On that first visit to Donaldson Correctional Facility my purpose was to observe the meditation classes being taught by inmates and then to interview some of them about their lives as prisoners.

The Houses of Healing course comes from a book by Robin Casarjian, the director of the Lionheart Foundation in Boston. Published in 1995, *Houses of Healing: A Prisoner's Guide to Inner Power and Freedom* is one of the tools that Lionheart provides for the rehabilitation of men and women in prison. Lionheart is also working towards a more rational approach to violence prevention, sentencing and incarceration in the U.S. This ground-breaking book caught the attention of inmate R. Troy Bridges while he was working in the Donaldson prison library. Troy had been incarcerated for more than ten years and was serving life without parole. After reading the book, which outlines a meditation-based program for personal recovery and healing, Troy and others began to meet as a study group, following the book's prescribed activities.

In 1996 Robin Casarjian received a letter from Bridges recounting the benefits he and others had derived from the regular practice of meditation. They had formed a core group which met every Thursday night to meditate in the tiny area next to his bunk in a crowded 100-man dormitory. "I have a bed by the window and three feet of space between the bed and the wall. I decided to temporarily move my bed away from the wall another two feet, and we could then sit on the floor and meditate. We spread blankets on the floor and were able to accommodate eight men. We have been meeting for over two months now, and every one of the original eight gives this weekly group meditation top priority. I noticed some of the rough edges of the personalities beginning to soften. They smile a little more, criticize a little less, and approach life in a calmer manner. We have all learned to use the noise and confusion of our adopted temple not as an annoyance but rather as our mantra."

After Bridges established a correspondence with Casarjian, the Lionheart Foundation began to provide guidance and assistance to the inmates and some prison staff by sending books, training manuals and, later, a videotape series used as a teaching tool for facilitators of the program. During the next six years more than 300 inmates at Donaldson participated in the Houses of Healing courses and support groups, initially under the tutelage of Bridges. Over time many more group facilitators were trained by Bridges and others, and they too began leading groups. From this pool of meditating inmates emerged a growing readiness to cultivate inner healing and wisdom through the practice of meditation.

I am not sure exactly what I expected would emerge from those first interviews with the meditating inmates at Donaldson. But as I met with the men one by one in the privacy of an office and taped them in long interviews, I found them opening up about their lives inside prison. What they told me was often surprising and remarkable, and listening to them changed my professional course in ways that I could not have anticipated.

I was deeply stirred by the power of their stories and the quandries they experience as men in prison. They live inside a dangerous social world in which there is incredible pressure to establish and demonstrate their manhood through aggressive behavior. They often feel compelled to join gangs and fight to prove dominance over one another. Violence, deprivation and stigmatization, in an environment of pervasive overcrowding and hopelessness, drive some men to an extreme acting out of perceived manhood-enhancing behaviors. Cut off from normal social avenues for constructing their reputation as men, these prisoners experience a need to publicly demonstrate their masculinity. In this depleted prison world their lives become a struggle to gather resources to build a reputation for strength and impregnability. They must show a readiness to fight to protect themselves and their possessions. The harsher the environment and more difficult the access to symbols of status and power, the more intense and protracted the battles become.

After meeting with the men at Donaldson and hearing them speak so frankly about prison life, I found them difficult to forget. I could not shake off the memories of what I had seen and heard. I wanted to learn more, to find out if there were solutions or alternatives to the aggressive culture of prison manhood. I wondered if it were possible for men in prison to live with a sense of inner peace and the freedom to experience and express a full range of emotions.

In my conversations with the inmates at Donaldson, they seemed to be seeking opportunities and skills to establish more productive and peaceful lives, even if there was no possibility of their release from prison. Perhaps this is because inmates face such difficult existential questions. They can either act out and distract themselves from the realities and consequences of their lives and crimes, or they can choose to face it all and try to make changes within themselves. Yet facing one's situation, really looking inward and focusing awareness upon the bleakness of incarceration, requires significant skills and guidance. I had already seen the benefits of teaching men in prison to meditate on an intermittent basis. But now I began to wonder if this approach offered them enough safety, privacy and direction to do this work in an environment with such high levels of distraction, stimulation and danger. After each meditation class prisoners must step right back into the daily stream of motion, noise and threats. I was searching for a way to provide prisoners with the sought-after safe space, extended time and specialized skills necessary to practice at a deeper, more lasting level of self-examination.

Sowing Seeds of Change

After my initial visit to Donaldson Correctional Facility in 1999, I sent two films to the prison psychologist, Dr. Ron Cavanaugh. The first, *Doing Time, Doing Vipassana*, (1997, Karuna Films Ltd.) tells the amazing story of the introduction in 1994 of a ten-day meditation program to 1,000 inmates at Tihar Jail, located outside New Delhi. With a total of 10,000 inmates, it is the largest prison in India. Tihar was once a site of violence, crime and overcrowding. Kiran Bedi, the prison warden, was looking for treatment programs that would address the serious psychological and social issues

Dr. Ron Cavanaugh

among the inmates. She had heard that S.N. Goenka, the renowned Vipassana meditation teacher, had been providing meditation courses at other Indian prisons since 1975. She decided to request Mr. Goenka to conduct a large Vipassana course at Tihar. This inspiring documentary shows the transformative power of prisoners systematically learning to develop deep inner awareness. It documents a reduction in violence and an improvement in the quality of life for a large prison population. Today there is a permanent Vipassana unit offering ongoing courses within Tihar.

The power of this film, coupled with the moving stories shared by the Donaldson inmates, had dominated my attention and energy since my visit there. I listened to their interviews over and over on the tape deck in my car and became convinced that the Vipassana program could provide the structure and approach for them to further address their personal suffering.

Doing Time, Doing Vipassana had already become an important factor in introducing the Vipassana meditation program to an American county jail. In 1997 the North Rehabilitation Facility (NRF), outside Seattle, Washington, held the first ten-day Vipassana course in a correctional facility in North America. Run by the King County Department of Public Health, NRF was a minimum-security jail specializing in substance abuse treatment for 300 inmates. As at Tihar, Vipassana courses became an established and active part of its curriculum. The program ran there for five years, until NRF was closed in 2002.

A two-year study conducted by its administrators (Meijer, 1999) demonstrated a significant reduction in recidivism for inmates participating in the Vipassana meditation courses compared to the overall rates at NRF. Subsequent research conducted by the Addictive Behaviors Research Center at the University of Washington, originally published in *American Jails* magazine (July 2003) and more recently in the journal *Psychology of Addictive Behaviors* (2006), demonstrated significant reductions in drug use, alcohol-related negative consequences and psychiatric symptoms, as well as increased optimism among the Vipassana participants three months after release from NRF.

The other film I sent to Ron Cavanaugh, *Changing from Inside* (1998, David Donnenfield Productions), documented these extraordinary transformations at NRF. Both films underscored for me that what is needed in prisons are treatment programs that teach a much deeper level of self-examination and mental training. When I sent these films to the Donaldson Correctional Facility, I felt as if I were sowing seeds of change. These seeds had already borne fruit in trials with diverse inmates in two dramatically different countries. What was still unclear was whether they could possibly take root and grow in the harsh and challenging environment at Donaldson.

The films slowly made their way throughout the prison, reaching a broad audience of both inmates and staff. Some inmates watched them over and over again. Several of the counselors in Road to Recovery, a federally funded therapeutic community within Donaldson, made the films available to their more than 200 inmate participants. A small but growing subculture of inmate meditators started to talk about the possibility of bringing a ten-day Vipassana course there. During the next year interest spread throughout the prison.

The importance these films had for many at Donaldson lay in their pertinence. Both address the issue of widespread human suffering and outline an approach for obtaining relief. This approach to misery is directly rooted in the experiences of Gotama the Buddha as he sought relief from his own suffering 2,600 years ago. The Buddha's enlightenment occurred when he figured out how a human being can purify his own mind and remove all causes of suffering. For those prisoners at Donaldson who were searching for deliverance from their troubled lives, the films demonstrated that this ancient method could be used by inmates today. The technique of Vipassana, essentially a set of guidelines for enlightened living, had now come front and center for the Donaldson inmates, considered among the most dangerous in North America and possibly beyond rehabilitation.

Introducing Vipassana

In Pali, the ancient language of the Buddha, Vipassana means "seeing things as they actually are." Vipassana meditation courses offer training in the precise technique taught by the Buddha for 45 years, 26 centuries ago in India.

Over a period of 500 years after the passing away of the Buddha, his complete teachings, known as the *Dhamma*, declined and were eventually lost to India. However, they survived in neighboring Myanmar (Burma) where they were passed intact from generation to generation among Buddhist monks, nuns and, eventually, lay people.

Vipassana was reintroduced to India in 1969 by S.N. Goenka, the Indian Burmese businessman and Vipassana adept who began offering courses there at the request of his own teacher, Sayagyi U Ba Khin. Soon people from around the world started joining the Indian students on these courses. Ten years later, Goenka began teaching farther abroad, and many of his students volunteered for activities that contributed to the globalization of this tradition. To date, more than 100 Vipassana meditation centers have been established in 26 countries, all offering the same courses on a donation-only basis for instruction, room and board. Thousands of people from 90 countries, from all walks of life, cultures and religions, as well as those following no religion, have since taken courses, guided by Mr. Goenka's instructions on audio and video recordings and trained assistant teachers on site.

On a course, usually of ten days, a student of Vipassana begins by undertaking five moral precepts as a necessary foundation for calming and concentrating the mind. He or she agrees to abstain from killing, stealing, false speech, taking intoxicants and sexual activity for the duration. Agreeing also to maintain "noble silence" (no communication with fellow students and only necessary communication with management and teachers), the meditator then works for three days on Anapana meditation, focusing awareness on the natural breath to sharpen the mind.

All of this is a preparation for learning Vipassana meditation. This technique involves the observation of ordinary, actual sensations throughout the body, moment by moment, and understanding their impermanent nature. A fundamental tenet of the Buddha's teachings is that bare attention or equanimous observation of what is actually happening within the mind/body each moment is, in and of itself, transformative and healing. Vipassana is the process of observing sensations and hence all mental contents (thoughts, emotions, etc.) without reacting.

As the practitioner develops more fully in this singular awareness, the experience of wisdom deepens. The observation of sensations gradually leads to an awareness of one's constant mental reactions to them. These reactions, which become conditioned attachments and addictions to one's feelings, beliefs and mental states, gradually diminish.

Dispassionate observation, without manipulation or control, is the aim. Whenever there is no reaction to current sensations, then unexplored, rejected and suppressed experiences can surface in the conscious mind and are similarly subjected to this therapeutic process of objective attention.

Incrementally, one overcomes deeply conditioned habitual reactions and emerges with a profound inner freedom and equanimity.

This approach—experiencing and observing one's misery with constancy and equanimity, looking at it squarely with patience and fortitude—is the path to experiential understanding and the liberation from suffering that many inmates (and others) seek. In the existentially threatening and demeaning prison environment, misery and identity crises prevail. The assumptions, multiple distractions and habits taken for granted in daily life outside prison are quickly stripped away. Inmates sit face to face with their destiny. They have plenty of time and plenty of misery. Donaldson inmates were now increasingly interested in learning how to use their time wisely to address their misery. Vipassana, for those who have the courage and motivation, offers a way, a path—the path of Dhamma.

Dhamma Takes Root

In January 2002, Donaldson Correctional Facility became the first state prison in North America to hold a Vipassana course. As the highest level maximum-security prison in Alabama, it is not entirely surprising that it agreed to try this innovative program. There is a sense at Donaldson that its inhabitants have reached the end of the line. Hopelessness, endemic throughout the burgeoning American penal system, affects nearly everyone at Donaldson, staff and inmates alike. It is severely understaffed, in part because it is the most difficult prison to recruit for in the state. Yet, in the center of this systemic stagnation lay ripeness for change. Ancient teachings for the cultivation of wisdom, recently revived in modern India and adapted by an American county jail, were now being considered by the administrators of the Alabama prison system with its widespread culture of overcrowded warehousing of inmates.

Frustrated with the lack of resources and the limitations inherent in meting out deterrence and punishment to inmates instead of rehabilitation, some of the staff were also drawn into the early excitement of bringing Vipassana to Donaldson. Two counselors in the drug recovery program, Denise Brickie and Bonita Johnson, continued to encourage the inmates to watch the Vipassana films. Ron Cavanaugh moved from his position as prison psychologist to become the director of treatment within the Alabama Department of Corrections. He was interested in bringing more treatment programs into the state's prisons. From that state-level vantage point, Ron became a champion of bringing Vipassana to Donaldson.

In January 2000, I contacted the Vipassana Meditation Center in Shelburne, Massachusetts, to explore the possibility of developing a Vipassana program within Donaldson. It was my good fortune to meet Jonathan Crowley, who for years had been interested in bringing Vipassana courses into American prisons and had volunteered on a minimum-security course at Seattle's King County jail (NRF). Over the next year and a half Jonathan and I brainstormed about the Donaldson project.

Soon after, Dr. Deborah Marshall, a former Alabama air force cadet and state trooper, joined the Donaldson staff as the new psychologist. As a practicing meditator, she immediately saw the value of this nascent project and became involved. Deborah, Jonathan and I began to conference-call every week and make more concrete plans. A year later Robin Casarjian and I proposed to Ron Cavanaugh that the Lionheart Foundation facilitate the implementation of a Vipassana program at Donaldson. With Ron's advocacy, this proposal was approved by the Alabama Department of Corrections.

In the spring of 2001, Deborah devoted herself to translating the principles of meditation into language understandable to the prison staff. With humor and determination she persisted in pushing the program forward. At morning staff meetings in Warden Bullard's office, she introduced ideas related to meditation and Vipassana. One morning she brought her meditation cushion and demonstrated for the staff how to sit in a meditation posture. Warden Bullard tried sitting on the cushion and assumed a beatific pose. Although he joked about the Vipassana program, he was clearly intrigued. He even began to express an interest in doing a ten-day course. With his active interest and acceptance, ideas and plans slowly took hold among prison staff.

The next step in establishing the program at Donaldson was to interest the most involved prison staff in undergoing a Vipassana meditation course. The Vipassana Prison Trust, a nonprofit organization that coordinates Vipassana programs within correctional settings, requires at least one administrator or treatment staff person to participate in a course. This is because prison staff must understand firsthand what is unique about Vipassana and its particular retreat set-up. Corrections personnel can then better help inmates to integrate their experiences after each course. Unless the staff have personally experienced the benefits of Vipassana for themselves, it is unlikely that a mere professional interest will sustain the effort needed to hold the courses and continue the program.

In June 2001, Warden Bullard sent Ron, Deborah and several Donaldson clinical and security staff to Massachusetts to do a ten-day retreat at the Vipassana Meditation Center (VMC). I met them at the Boston airport, and we all drove to Shelburne and participated in the course together. Now that a core group of staff had experienced the course and were practicing Vipassana meditation, the groundwork had been laid to introduce the program to inmates at the prison.

I flew to Alabama that October with two Vipassana teachers, Jonathan Crowley and Rick Crutcher, a student of Pali who was the only western teacher to participate in the historic 1,000-inmate course at Tihar Prison in India. We spent several days at Donaldson with Warden Bullard, Deborah and Ron planning the details of their first Vipassana prison program and meeting with a group of 30 interested inmates.

During this visit we showed the film *Doing Time, Doing Vipassana* to the inmates. Most of them had already seen it and many knew the film by heart. They were particularly curious to meet and observe Jonathan and Rick, the "free-world" men they had heard about who wanted to spend ten days living and teaching inside the prison. As one man later expressed it, "We thought they were going to be freaks since we heard they wanted to come to prison."

The inmates had many questions about the course. Some wondered if they were prepared and knowledgeable enough about meditation to take the course. They were told that the course requires no prior experience, just an informed interest, and is designed equally for beginners and others with some experience. One man, Edward Johnson, worried about his suppressed anger, fearing that it might overwhelm him if he slowed down and looked inward. Rick assured him that he would be taught the skills and given the guidance he needed, and told him that coming face to face with his anger was the precise healing work that he needed to do. Edward later remembered that initial conversation with Rick as a personal turning point which convinced him, although still filled with trepidation, to attend the Vipassana course.

The prison's gymnasium would be set up as a separate, locked meditation unit for the 20 students and three volunteer staff: Rick Crutcher was to be the course teacher; Bruce Stewart would join Jonathan Crowley as course managers.

Their ten-day stay would be the first time "free-world" men lived around the clock among inmates inside a North American maximum-security prison. Their living arrangements were based on the competing rules and regulations of a Vipassana course and a prison. For reasons of security and because of a strict code that separates prisoners from the rest of society, non-inmates are not allowed to live inside a prison. Normally, of course, there are no requests to do this. In accordance with this code of strict separation, prisoners live only with other prisoners and with corrections officers and have very little contact with outsiders.

By contrast, at all Vipassana courses in nonprison settings, it is essential that the meditation instructors and support staff live among and serve the meditation students within the same residential setting. As we planned this first Vipassana course at Donaldson, it was now imperative that some way be found which would allow the teacher and managers to live inside among their inmate students.

This seemingly insurmountable impasse was resolved by the warden who made an exception to the rule because he was impressed with the Vipassana group's mission. An architectural anomaly at Donaldson also helped make this possible. Within the gymnasium is a small, unoccupied security post reached by a narrow, iron staircase. This airless room, with an open toilet and windows overlooking the gymnasium floor, could accommodate the teacher and managers. Warden Bullard agreed to reverse the established policy on the condition that the three men would sleep locked in this separate area above the gym. We were all touched by this demonstration of his trust in the program.

We also had to discuss the logistics of rearranging the gymnasium into a temporary Vipassana center. The warden offered to provide some extra carpeting from his own house for the floor of the proposed "meditation hall" area and use of a nearby prison staff house for the preparation of the vegetarian food required for the course students and its staff.

At the end of these meetings we set a date for the opening of the program in mid-January 2002. We were on our way.

Setting Up the Vipassana Retreat

In the days immediately before the ten-day retreat, the gymnasium, normally a site of noise and activity, was transformed into a meditation refuge. During the Vipassana course the gymnasium became a separate restricted area, a safe, quiet place for the inmate-students to eat, sleep and meditate in total seclusion from the rest of prison society. By its very nature, a prison is a separate and restricted place. It is also an involuntary place, built for the purpose of restraining a population considered harmful to those outside of its boundaries. Ironically, the gymnasium was now being converted into a voluntary refuge for the benefit and protection of those within its boundaries. In essence, the gym was being fashioned into a monastery of sorts within the walls of a maximum-security prison. While there, the inmates were to be considered and treated akin to cloistered monks.

The protected, secluded status of the Vipassana students was distinctly different from their normal role as prison inmates. Prisoners are familiar with the enforced seclusion of the "hole," or solitary confinement, known as segregation at Donaldson. There they are separated both from society and the general prison population as a form of punishment or for the protection of other inmates and staff. But the seclusion of the Vipassana site altered the hierarchical notion of prisoners as an underclass. As Vipassana students, they were to be segregated for their own benefit, to protect their silent introspection from noise and interference. This change in status allowed them to shed their role as inmates and begin to move into a more expansive identity and consciousness.

By suspending tarpaulins with wires from ceiling brackets, the prison maintenance crew, with the active help of several inmates who would be undertaking the course, transformed the large, open gymnasium into three separate areas for sleeping, eating and meditating. Windows facing a small, enclosed yard were blocked with cardboard to ensure privacy for the meditators from the potentially distracting and prying gaze of general population inmates.

Tables, chairs, pots, pans and cooking supplies were borrowed from various prison departments. Other supplies for the course poured in from the local area and from farther away: Deborah Marshall's meditation group in Birmingham lent their meditation cushions; a carpenter from Seattle built a small, collapsible version of the traditional wooden teacher's seat and shipped it to Donaldson; the kitchen manager from the meditation center in Shelburne sent a rice cooker.

An air of excitement, possibility and cooperative energy began to fill the gymnasium. When the room was ready, one student said, "Prior to Vipassana, you could feel the negative emotions bouncing off the walls in this place. After we got it prepared, it was no longer a gymnasium. It had something holy about it." Another exclaimed, "This place doesn't look like prison."

Throughout the prison, staff and inmates alike were placing bets on how many of the 20 registered students would remain at the end of the ten days. Most predicted that the lure of mail, phone and television or the arduous schedule of self-denial and self-reflection would be too much. Many of

The gym, transformed into a meditation site

the students were nervous and filled with misgivings, wondering what they would encounter when they looked deeply within and faced the consequences of past mistakes. They were risking being overwhelmed by their own negative emotions or flooded by memories of past trauma. They had been assured that they would receive the help and attention they needed to do the inner, meditative work. They had also agreed to give up the scant but cherished privileges of a prison inmate for the duration of the course. They could not buy any items from the prison canteen nor maintain contact with the outside world by phone, mail or family visits.

For the men, this had created a new sense of loss, a fear of additional erosion of their ties to society and loved ones, and the dread that they might be forgotten forever. In return for these significant sacrifices, they hoped to gain the safety, security and guidance required to complete this intensive, demanding retreat from the world in which they lived. They were clearly taking a gamble. So too were Warden Bullard and Ron Cavanaugh. Everyone knew that this program was historic and that the potential for future programs rested upon their collective shoulders. They all felt the burden of this speculation and attention.

Free Worlders Move Inside

Over the weekend before the start of the course, everyone involved assembled at the prison staff house. Deborah Marshall was to oversee the course as it unfolded from moment to moment. Her purview included the students, the course staff, the three rotating corrections officers who were asked to provide security in the gym, and the interface between the program and the prison. I would be cooking for the course at the staff house kitchen under the guidance of Roy Milwid, an experienced Vipassana course and kitchen manager from Canada. We made plans to handle the complicated logistics of cooking in one location and then transporting everything by van, transferring it all onto a food trolley to go through the security system into the prison and finally into the gymnasium, three times a day.

On the morning of January 14, 2002, after staying for several days at the prison staff house, Jonathan, Rick and Bruce packed their bags and drove down the road to the prison. They knew that they would not be leaving Donaldson Correctional Facility for ten days. Like the inmate students, they were going to be locked inside the gymnasium with no access to the outside world.

Although this first Vipassana course in a state prison was the fulfillment of a longstanding dream for the Vipassana volunteers, they were apprehensive. Rick and Jonathan had participated in the courses at the county jail in Seattle, but those courses were held in a low-security facility with a population whose average length of stay was one year. The stereotypes and projections about maximum-security prisons and their inhabitants, heightened by media coverage of high profile crimes and prison violence, created some last minute anxiety. At a Donaldson security briefing they were told, "These guys are nice, but they can kill you."

On that Monday evening, the 20 Vipassana students moved into their newly constructed refuge. This short walk represented a huge change in their lives as prisoners. Hauling their plastic-covered prison mattresses and laundry bags of white prison uniforms down the hallway, they

Inmates move mattresses and requisites to the gym

entered the converted gym. In the moments just before the door was locked, many of them experienced doubt and fear.

During an orientation meeting held just before the official start of the course, to everyone's surprise and relief, both inmates and teachers relaxed. Bruce remembers that, "The guys had bright sparkling eyes, and when they smiled, they communicated warmth." Jonathan, who was to orient the inmates to the rules of the retreat, was concerned about how he would be viewed and whether he would be taken seriously by guys who are characterized as big, strong and aggressive. The inmates wondered about these men from the "free world" who would choose to be locked inside a prison gymnasium with them for ten days. One of the inmates asked, "Are you guys afraid of us? You don't look afraid!"

According to Jonathan, that question was a turning point: Initial tensions subsided as the inmates saw the confidence that he and Bruce had in them and their decisions to undertake the challenging Vipassana program. Once this statement was out in the open, everyone could laugh and acknowledge that there had been a mutual testing and scrutiny of one another. "There were fears about going into a maximum-security prison to be with inmates, many of whom had been there for decades," Jonathan said. "The remarkable thing was to go into this stereotyped, oppressive environment and to see that these guys are just human. All the barriers dropped away. They were just students meditating. We never again referred to them as inmates."

Similarly, the students felt increasingly comfortable and reassured by their interactions with the course leaders and realized that they were in safe and skillful hands. Over the next ten days, offering an unending supply of dedication, care and warmth, the three men became their trusted mentors.

Each night the corrections officer on duty locked Rick, Bruce and Jonathan inside the small security station above the gym. The three men referred to their room as "the bridge" because of the similarity in location and function to the bridge of a ship. Resting on their plastic prison mattresses on the floor, they talked about their students and how each one was faring. If a particular student's spirits were flagging, or if a student was experiencing emotional "storms" or

Rick   Jonathan   Bruce

having physical ailments, the men shared their impressions, concerns and remedies. In Bruce's words, "What was remarkable was that we were there in this deadened environment, all concrete, with minimal accoutrements, and there was something so alive happening. In the center of this noisy, chaotic prison, the silence and focused meditation changed the feel of the gymnasium. We were continuously excited about every little thing that happened during those ten days."

In the early hours of their stay, Rick, Bruce and Jonathan established themselves in their prescribed roles. These roles are maintained at all Vipassana courses and were closely adhered to at Donaldson. As the teacher, Rick's main responsibility was to preserve an atmosphere of loving encouragement. He was present and meditating along with the students during all meditation sessions. While silence is strictly required among the students for the first nine days of the course, they do speak with the teacher about their meditation. Rick would check on each student's progress during short, daily interviews at the front of the meditation hall. The students could also sign up for private meetings with him if they had a question about how their meditation was going. Every evening Rick played a video lecture by

S.N. Goenka in which he articulates the philosophical underpinnings of the students' day-by-day experiences and provides healthy and necessary injections of humor and encouragement. Although Rick was out of sight during the breaks from meditation and for meals, he never left the confines of the refuge. Throughout the course his active listening and counseling skills were essential to the students' welfare and personal growth.

In contrast to Rick's role, course managers live closely among the students and become involved when necessary in the nitty-gritty details of their lives. Students can talk with the course managers any time, day or night, about important, unmet physical requirements.

The three men already knew that these students, because they were prisoners, would need more nurturing, reassurance and encouragement than students on regular courses. A conscious decision was made at the start to have Bruce and Jonathan stay in close verbal contact with them as they settled into their cloistered life. Right away the managers felt the tentative reaching out from them, the search for the reassurance needed in order to feel trust and safety. In response, Bruce and Jonathan watched over and cared for the students in all aspects of their lives, cleaning the toilets, laying out the returned laundry, and buttering their toast.

By ministering to their emotional and physical needs with compassion, the managers were enabling the students to give attention to the intensely demanding inner work. In Bruce's words, "We were total strangers coming into their prison and representing some kind of authority figures. There was a lot of trust- and confidence-building that had to go on before and during the early days of the course. As we began to work with these guys, they would come up to us and make casual remarks or ask a question. We could see they were warming up to us and

Sleeping cubicles created inside the gym

testing the waters. This prepared them so they could come to us later on as their storms and crises arose during the course." After many years of building walls around their feelings, these students needed to be sure that this was a safe place to open up, experience and expose suppressed emotions and memories. Over the next ten days, like dormitory parents in a boarding school, Bruce and Jonathan were immediately and attentively present to the students 24 hours a day. Although not directly involved on this level, Rick watched over the students very closely and had long discussions with Bruce and Jonathan about the men late into the night.

Everyone working on this first maximum-security Vipassana course strongly believed that a prison, under the right conditions, could provide an environment which is conducive to intensive inner work. In prison there are few of the distractions typically found in the outside world. In Bruce's words, "At Vipassana centers we often describe the environment we create as that of a prison. When possible, we provide returning students with individual "cells" as they become ready for increased solitude. Prisons already have this cloistered environment. Whether the door is locked or not is really irrelevant. The purpose of all this is to provide an environment in which one can accept each moment as it comes and deal with what really enslaves you."

The three corrections officers (COs) assigned to the Vipassana course worked in rotating eight-hour shifts. Early on in the course, Jimmie Jackson, one of the staff who had taken the ten-day course in Massachusetts, Terry Thomas and Mitch Etheridge—known as "Big E"—became the self-appointed defenders of the students from any threats, ridicule or misunderstanding. Rather than maintaining their normal security function—watching the inmates so they didn't cause problems or escape from the

Mitch Etheridge, "Big E"

gymnasium—the three COs were essentially on guard so that no one on the outside could break through the protective bubble of silence and stillness established there and disturb the students. These tall, heavy-set African American men became increasingly involved in and committed to shielding and advocating for the inmates in their special, vulnerable state as monastic students.

One day Big E was accompanying several of the students down an open prison corridor on their way to the secluded yard set aside for the program's daily walking periods. These scheduled, supervised breaks were the only times the students could choose to leave the confines of the gymnasium. Another corrections officer stepped menacingly toward the group and spoke loudly to them, declaring, "Remember, this is my hallway. Take off your hats!" Normally, this incident wouldn't be at all noteworthy in the course of daily prison life. Firm rules and restrictions are grist for the mill in providing "security." However, the role reversal in the Vipassana course meant that the inmates themselves were in need of security and protection from the everyday abrasiveness of the corrections officer. In response, Big E immediately herded his charges into the yard and then let the CO know that his very typical behavior toward the inmates could not be tolerated in this case. Later, when one of the inmate students said he did not want to use yard time anymore because of this incident, he was assured that steps had been taken to prevent this from recurring. The temporary modification in the role of the CO from security to advocacy and protection for inmates was another of the cultural adjustments made to accommodate the Vipassana course.

Working Deep Within

On the first day of the course the men were awakened by a gong at 4: 00 a.m. Throughout the ten days this gong, rung by Bruce or Jonathan, would punctuate the silence to announce the strictly timed routines of meditating, eating, taking breaks and sleeping. That first morning, without a sound, the students filed to their assigned meditation cushions in the "meditation hall" at the far end of the gymnasium, separated from the sleeping

Notice board, area for shoes

area by the suspended tarps. The basketball hoops had been covered with white cloth, and all indications of sports activities were hidden from sight. The transformation from gymnasium to monastery was complete. The students sat down to begin their journey inside. Rick soon joined them, sitting cross-legged on a raised seat in front of them.

Over the next three days, for eleven hours a day, all of the men were directed in the practice of Anapana meditation, the systematic observation of the breath as it enters and exits the nostrils. Wrapped in blankets, with white knitted prison caps atop their heads, the men sat as much as possible in absolute quiet and stillness. Outside the door to the refuge, normal prison activity swept and swirled up and down the halls. Sounds of shouting, banging, clanking and jangling only distantly intruded into the cloistered atmosphere. The transformed gymnasium was imbued with an air of reverence and sober work. The students were struck by the unfamiliar silence and by their combined energies as they tried not to move. During those initial three days they were making the transition from an externally focused, noisy, chaotic, dangerous world to their solitary uncharted worlds within.

Anapana, the ancient Pali word meaning awareness of respiration, is the first important skill taught in a Vipassana course. For three days the student sits and focuses on the area below the nostrils, above the upper lip, noticing the sensations of the breath as it moves in and out of the body. This is bare observation of the natural breath from moment to moment. It is not a technique to change the breath. No use is made of any mantras or visualizations or objects of focus which could soothe the emotions and simplify the task of developing concentration. Such aids build up a dependence on something created, imaginary or external. As one sits, hour after hour, the mind may go wild with thoughts, feelings and manufactured distractions. Students learn that the breath is an important bridge between the conscious and the unconscious mind. Anapana practice teaches the mind to become calm and sharply focused and the body to become still. Using this breath observation the student gradually develops an anchoring skill that can help him face the deeper emotional storms and passions that emerge later. Eventually, with persistence and guidance, the effects of Anapana are realized, and the student is ready to go deeper within.

For many, this was the first time in their lives that they had sat still for any length of time. In this society, sitting still is not a particularly valued skill unless it is in front of a TV or computer. It is even more unusual in a prison, where incessant stimuli—the sights, sounds and stench—and strong emotions of fear, dread, loss and grief rarely foster feelings of peace or calm. The men were now facing all their usual preferences and routines, squirming and struggling against their desire to move and escape. They ached for their normal habits and distractions, and many had thoughts of dropping out of the course. These are very common reactions experienced by students on all Vipassana courses.

The presence of Rick, Bruce and Jonathan meditating on mats in front of them also helped to hold them there. The three experienced Vipassana practitioners were no longer seen as weird; they were just right there with them, doing exactly what they were instructing the students to do. Vipassana was not a "prisoners' activity" being imposed on them by those in control. Instead, the three men were modeling and intimately sharing meditation with them as is done for students on all courses. This ancient inner process was alive and tangible

Inmate-meditators and Jonathan

and unfolding right in front of and inside of them, and the students were curious and heartened by what they saw and felt. As time passed they became increasingly intrigued and committed to staying.

In the early days of the course, Anapana developed into a significant life tool for the students, one that they could use in the heat of the moment during a crisis or in a planned and systematic way during times of quiet reflection. It placed at their disposal a powerful link between inner and outer reality, and gave them a map for their inward journey.

On the fourth day, guided by the audio instructions of Mr. Goenka, the students started the practice of Vipassana meditation. They began to direct their sharpened awareness systematically throughout the entire body in a prescribed way, observing bodily sensations as they moved their awareness from head to toes and back again. After three days of focusing awareness on the breath in a limited area, this shift to the whole body can be liberating but can also uncover and release strong emotions.

According to Bruce, "With the practice of Vipassana, you begin to realize on an experiential level that there is no separation between the mind and the body. All the past conditioning that we carry with us is really locked in the body. As you observe the sensations some very unpleasant memories and strong emotions begin to arise, along with a lot of aches and pains. The unlocking of these memories, physical sensations and emotions produces what we refer to as storms, or waves of reactivity. We guide the student through these storms so they can discover experientially that, regardless of how deep and horrible and painful a storm might be, mentally, physically and emotionally, everything is constantly changing, arising and passing away."

During this turbulent but ultimately healing journey, the student of Vipassana must sit tight and hold on with as much equanimity as possible through the wild unfolding of physical and emotional pain. The relationship between dukkha, the pervasive suffering and unsatisfactory nature of life, and anicca, the constantly changing, impermanent, ephemeral characteristic of life, is central to the teachings of the Buddha. Through Vipassana this dialectic becomes a personally experienced reality. When a storm passes and calm returns, the wisdom gained from experiencing it out in a more balanced way lends a fresh perspective about the origins of and the solutions to one's own suffering.

In the long, solitary hours of meditation, the students discovered that there are times of bliss and peace when the body seems to dissolve into a mass of vibrations referred to as "free flow." At other times, the body is wracked with physical and psychic pain. One student, Omar Rahman, recalled that on the fourth day, "I was sitting, wrestling with the pain in my body and trying to figure out a way to be at peace with it. All of a sudden I started shaking all over. This was totally different from my shaking during Anapana. I was sitting on a volcano, trying to ride it, and I refused to get off because I was going somewhere." Today Omar believes that his powerful mind/body experience of pain was a breakthrough. "It was like I cleaned myself of something. Something deeply buried came up out of me, and now I feel so much better." According to Jonathan, "After going through an emotional storm with Vipassana, you realize that there is no experience that is going to make you permanently happy. There is no experience that is going to make you permanently sad. Equanimity is achieving this wisdom and accepting everything just as it is from moment to moment."

After beginning the practice of Vipassana meditation, many days of storms and struggles lay ahead for the students. Right from the start it became clear to Bruce, Rick and Jonathan that these men were exceptional in the level of commitment and fortitude they brought to battle their demons, as well as in their collective desire to cultivate equanimity and wisdom. The three men agreed that in teaching and managing regular Vipassana courses they had not come across more serious and determined students. The inmates seemed to work harder; in fact, they were at times told to back off and ease up on themselves. Many leaped into their meditation with such intensity and gusto that the three guides were concerned that they would become

In silent meditation, nine of the ten days

exhausted or overwhelmed, unable to finish the course. They wondered if it was the nature of the setting and situation that drove these students to dig so forcefully. Was a high security prison more conducive to the training in self-wisdom than freer and more fortunate circumstances?

As the course unfolded, Rick, Bruce and Jonathan searched for reasons that explained why these students were so devoted to their new practice. They concluded that it was the students' preexisting level of suffering and their search for answers and solutions to the existential predicament of being in prison that led them so strongly into the inner work. In Bruce's words, "These guys already knew suffering so profoundly and blatantly. They were under no illusion that they were happy. They knew from the start that they were miserable. But they didn't yet know why they were miserable. Now, through meditation, they discovered that they were not, as they had thought, victims of society but were primarily victims of themselves. They began to look at what really enslaves them. They learned to be in the present, to face the present moment at the level of sensations and to accept that moment. Vipassana gave them the tools to face, at a deep level, all that misery inside. And when you really face all that stuff, what is left after the storm is peace and equanimity."

As the men rode out their storms, hour after hour, Jonathan, Bruce and Rick watched over them. At night from "the bridge" they could look down on the sleeping area, two rows of mattresses on the floor separated by bedsheets strung

Alone in silence, together in meditation

on wires. They could see at a glance whether everyone was asleep. Some men experienced insomnia or nightmares. Others had diarrhea as their intestinal systems adapted to the first fruit and dairy products they had had since entering prison years earlier. (Since inmates at Donaldson had at one time used fruit to manufacture "julep," an alcoholic beverage, it was no longer allowed in the prison diet.) Others were initially constipated from the long hours of sitting. No matter what struggles arose, the three men found treatments and relief in order to comfort the students, thereby allowing them to devote their attention to the inner work.

During the middle days of the course, as emotions and passions surface, ordinary events of daily life on the course can become saturated with significance. A simple object or occurrence can unlock waves of reactivity and reverberate throughout the hours and days of meditation. Usually this was privately played out on a solitary meditation cushion. If emotions became too strong to continue with the practice of Vipassana, the students were instructed to return to the more grounding Anapana meditation. At times other students and staff noticed sobs, grimaces or a sudden flight from the meditation hall to the bathroom or sleeping area. Bruce or Jonathan sometimes needed to guide and encourage a distressed student back to the meditation mat with helpful reminders about the practice: "The process is working. Work with Anapana for some time. Welcome your stuff coming up." Time after time these simple, whispered reassuring encounters reset the course for the students. They were told, in the heat and anguish of storms of feeling, that those same intense emotions which they had avoided and warded off over a lifetime were in fact the gateway to their peace and happiness. These gentle instructions became crystallized moments of learning that enabled them to sit still and persist in their work.

All 20 students have their own Vipassana stories, tales of storms and intense perseverance followed by individual resolution and realization. Woven through these tales are the common patterns and themes of the Vipassana process. Their personal experiences became odysseys of valor. Prison is an everyday battleground fraught with drama and high stake quests. In Vipassana, the students were afforded a brief reprieve from the chaos and pandemonium of incarceration. Away from their usual external enemies, locked inside the gymnasium and seated on their meditation mats, they faced the most challenging battles of all.

Within this silent refuge there grew an intense shared devotion and collectivity that knit everyone together. Prison normally isolates and alienates one from another. Solidarity was a fresh experience for the students, strengthening their receptivity and dogged commitment to the course. Each individual was doing his own work alone in the crowd. Yet the group was a fraternity in the making, a brotherhood of experience, intensely individual as far as each man's life and history went but shared at a deeper level by their mutual observation of the timeless and universal truths of impermanence and suffering.

THE DHAMMA BROTHERS

This is a story about the power of and the potential for personal and social change among inmates inside a maximum-security prison. The individual stories of these men as they participated in the Vipassana course challenge all the common assumptions and stereotypes about prisoners as society's rejects for whom nothing works, or as parasites who live off public funds, watch television all day and have no interest in self-improvement. The inmates in the Vipassana course threw themselves into this intensely challenging program with such avidity and courage that it seemed as if their very survival depended upon completing the course.

The visual image of 20 inmates meditating in silence and stillness, hour after hour, day after day, will forever stay with me. Perhaps these inmates were somewhat unusual because they made the effort to sign up for the program. But they were not chosen from among any elite inmate ranks, and no incentives were offered. They were simply prisoners seeking treatment. They each sought out, considered and ultimately chose this course of action for their own personal reasons and by their own free will.

Who were the men behind these criminal records and long sentences? In letters often written and sent amid frustrating circumstances, in interviews arranged under endless bureaucratic stipulations and in hard-to-come-by special visits, the Dhamma Brothers, as they came to call themselves, willingly shared their lives in the hope that someone would listen. Here are their own very personal stories, the stories of the Dhamma Brothers.

Grady Bankhead

Grady Bankhead has a sentence of life without the possibility of parole. Now in his fifties, he has been incarcerated for over 20 years, on death row for the first eight. His crime was to stand by and witness a murder. Although Grady did not commit the crime, he drove the getaway car, leaving the scene with the murderers. Tried as a capital crime and sentenced to death in the electric chair, Grady narrowly escaped execution. In a retrial defended by Attorney Bryan Stevenson of Equal Justice Initiative, Grady was released from the death sentence and given life without parole.

Grady has struggled over the years to accept his fate while watching his family lose touch with him. "Life without parole means that you are to be warehoused until you die. It doesn't mean that you are to be punished, or worked, or any of that. It means that they don't want you back in society. What it meant to me was just a longer way to die than the electric chair. I thought the judge just wanted me to grow old and die. I wanted to get it over with because my family was suffering."

When he was five years old, one day Grady's mother dressed him and his three-year-old brother, Danny, in their best clothes, drove them out into the countryside and left them on the porch of an old abandoned house at the end of a long driveway. She instructed them to stay on the porch, that Grady was to take care of Danny and that she would be back to get them. After standing there all night Grady climbed down and found an old hubcap filled with rainwater. He also found a dead bird. These were the rations that kept the boys alive. Their mother never returned. In the days following their abandonment, Grady tried to care for Danny, who had a weak heart and had always been frail. But they were not found for several days. Danny later died, and Grady was filled with guilt about his death. Rather than blaming his mother, whom he didn't see again until he got to death row, he always blamed himself.

In a similar way Grady has blamed himself about the murder he witnessed. He has experienced tremendous anger and a sense of restlessness about his incarceration. The fear of fully facing and experiencing his anger made him reluctant to sign up for the Vipassana course. But during the course he was able to look at the crime in a deeper way, experience the underlying grief and finally come to a sense of self-forgiveness. "Until then I had actually justified and excused myself for the crime. During Vipassana I just couldn't get away from myself. I had to see it. And one of the things Vipassana teaches you is any negative behavior starts within. The misery starts in here. Then it carries somewhere else. So I'm guilty, even though I never hit the man. Now I don't have to make excuses to myself anymore. I pulled some of my masks off. In my other treatments, I never have been able to do that."

Grady says that the Vipassana program has helped him accept prison as his home. "So today, this is my home. They may transfer me to another prison, and then that is my home. But I'm all right living here." This resolve to make prison his home and to peacefully accept that reality was sorely tested last year. Grady found out from another inmate, who had seen the story on TV, that his daughter Brandy had been brutally murdered by a man in a motel room. The terrible details of this crime, coupled with his inability to respond to or seek solace from his family, were an incredible test of Grady's inner strength. But his inclusion in the Dhamma brotherhood and his reliance upon his Vipassana practice provided a source of support.

Torrence Barton

Torrence Barton is in his twenties. Born in Montgomery, Alabama, he and two sisters were raised by their mother and never knew their father. Searching for a father figure, Torrence strayed from home, embracing people he thought exemplified strength. He dropped out of high school in the tenth grade. In an attempt to better his living conditions he pursued fast money, which ultimately led to his incarceration. His mother died while he was in prison. This was a huge loss for him, and he keeps a photograph of her over his bed. Torrence writes poetry now and aspires to write his life story. "Bondage in my eyes stems from the avoidance of reality and the embracing of illusions. Facing life as it really is leads to freedom from the two." He attended the Vipassana course and then, four years later, the three-day refresher course, in order to participate in a "constructive endeavor." He says, "Vipassana meditation is a practice I'm using while residing in this contaminated womb. The practice has become one of my most productive tools against a stillborn delivery becoming my fate. I've learned that through consistent practice, I can receive proper nourishments that aid me."

Michael Carpenter

Michael Carpenter is a tall, lanky man in his thirties. Seventeen years ago he was convicted of homicide and sentenced to life without parole. Michael's mother was 20 years old when he was born, and his grandparents raised him from infancy in Huntsville, Alabama. He never knew his biological father. When Michael was a teenager his grandfather became increasingly abusive. At the age of seventeen he ran away from home and hid in a nearby wooded area, moving among various abandoned houses and hiding from the police. He later moved in with a girlfriend and her mother, but before long he was drawn into drug use and dealing. The next year, along with his girlfriend and a friend, he was convicted of the capital murder of a local drug dealer.

During the Vipassana course Michael met with his feelings of regret and the reality that he faces a lifetime in prison. After many days of tears and overwhelming grief, he realized that his hatred of his situation was causing him such deep, self-inflicted suffering that he was not making a healthy adjustment to prison. Sitting with and fully experiencing this realization has allowed him to feel more peaceful and to cultivate a sense of resolution. Michael recently sat a second Vipassana course and continues his daily practice.

Willie Carroll

Willie Carroll has been in prison for the past 26 years. He was born in Birmingham, Alabama. When he was five years old his mother left him in the care of his father. He never saw her again. Suddenly losing his mother at such a young age deeply troubled him, and throughout his early teens Willie became increasingly unmanageable. When he was 14 his older sister Pearl brought him to Dayton, Ohio. Pearl was then a young mother of three small children and, although she tried to integrate Willie into her family, he rebelled against her authority. He began to steal bikes and roam a nearby shopping mall, stealing from stores. Two years later Willie stole a car from a dealership and headed back to Birmingham. On the way he stole fuel from gas stations, but he was arrested and never made it home. At 16 he was sent to adult prison. Desperate to go home, he tried several times to escape. Now 44 years old, Willie has been imprisoned more than half his life.

Once Willie stopped trying to escape and settled down to the reality of a long prison sentence, he began to reach out for help. He worked hard in the available prison treatment programs and has lived and worked in the drug recovery unit at Donaldson since 1998. When he heard about Vipassana in 2002, he quickly signed up even though he was filled with fear of "the garbage that is going to come up."

"To this date, Vipassana has offered and continues to bring peace of mind to me, even and especially in times of seemingly total despair. I've learned to adjust my way of thinking to life as it is and not as wanted. Twice I have done the course of Vipassana at Donaldson, and twice I've gotten more and more close to being able to feel myself grow more spiritual, get a little more freer than before. I still sit and meditate daily. On Saturdays I sit with the group for a couple hours. When I get out of prison I plan on doing a ten-day course with my sister Pearl."

Wayne Finch

Wayne Finch has been incarcerated at Donaldson with a homicide conviction since 1998. At the age of ten he began to roam the streets of Aniston, Alabama, drinking, smoking and stealing from stores. His mother, a single parent who was a nurse at the local hospital, was unable to control his behavior. A few years later he joined a gang and began to steal cars and sell drugs. After frequent stays in state lockup facilities for youth, he was tried as an adult in 1985 and sent to prison at the age of sixteen. Prison only helped him cultivate his reputation as a fighter. Whether inside prison or on the streets, Wayne was into illegal activities.

Under the supervision of correctional officer "Big E," Finch, now in his thirties, manages the prison sports programs. Over the years he had frequently received disciplinary reports, and when he decided to enter the Vipassana course both his fellow inmates and the prison staff were skeptical about Finch's ability to settle down and do the intense work that would be required of him. Bruce remembers that "Wayne seemed very much shut down to the world. His body language was very stiff, very defiant."

Once the course got under way Wayne became withdrawn, unable to do the work. Jonathan and Bruce made an extra effort to reach out to him, but he remained aloof and preoccupied. Rick noticed that he squirmed and fidgeted on the mat, and he guessed that Wayne was blocking, or defending himself against, the internal process. He diligently stuck with his meditation on the breath but avoided going deeper. One day, when Bruce sat next to him at lunch, Wayne mumbled, "I can't go there. I can't face this. There are things that shouldn't have happened."

On the sixth day, during the lunch break, Rick had a pivotal meeting with him. "Wayne was frightened," said Rick, "and clearly trying to ward off his "stuff." My advice seemed perfunctory at the time, but I realize now how valuable it was. I told him he was in a critical place and that this had happened because of the hard efforts he had made with Anapana meditation. Something had risen to the surface of his mind, and there was only one way to get past it. I told him that he needed to begin working with the sensations on the body if he was going to be able to come to terms with these issues. Otherwise it would be difficult to stay in the course because he was experiencing too much tension."

Wayne's painful situation was only being heightened by the avoidance of his suffering. All the violence of his past was right in his face. With Vipassana, he had the opportunity to move toward the acceptance of the reality of his suffering. He had always kept himself in motion, running from his troubled past. Rick explained to Wayne, "Facing reality, just as it is, is the path to freedom. Sensations on the body are the tool to bring it up, to accept it and then to gain equanimity. Once you face it, it no longer enslaves you."

After the meeting with Rick, Wayne returned to the meditation cushion with a new openness. On the eighth day Wayne's attitude of withdrawal disappeared, and he began to complain openly: He didn't like the food; he didn't like the routine. His complaints, however, seemed to be his way of connecting, of making contact with Bruce and Jonathan, of engaging with his surroundings. Appreciating this, Bruce and Jonathan patiently listened to his complaints. Later that day Bruce noticed Wayne crouching down in a corner of the dining area, kicking and blowing at something. Bruce eventually went over and asked what he was doing. Wayne explained that he was helping a spider back into its web.

Bruce noted, "His whole body language had changed. He was changing." The three mentors realized with some relief that Wayne was now fully engaged and would be able to stay for the entire course. On the tenth day, immediately after silence was broken among the students, Wayne confided in Bruce about a traumatic event that had been intolerable for him to acknowledge consciously. In Bruce's words, "This was a huge breakthrough for Wayne. He was finally able to face this horrible thing that he had been attempting to deal with by shutting down and rebelling and acting tough. Vipassana takes you to that level where you simply have to face things. Wayne was able to do this through his own efforts in his own way."

James George

James George is in his fifties and has been under lock and key for 31 of the past 35 years. His father was a bootlegger who made and sold whiskey. "I began drinking when I was nine and became introduced to drugs at 15. I went to prison at 16 and, since May 1966, I have spent all but 25 months incarcerated." Although never charged with a violent crime, longstanding drug addictions and drug-related crimes have prevented him from sustaining himself outside prison.

In the early hours of the Vipassana course James discovered an inner self that habitual drug and alcohol use had blocked from his awareness. He meditated with such dedication that he was reluctant to take breaks, rest or go to meals. James was always the first on the cushion in the early morning hours and the last to leave in the evening. One day James approached Bruce with a smile and said, "If it gets any better than this, I don't know if I can stand it." Because of his fervent attachment to meditation, Bruce and Jonathan wondered whether James could sustain his intense level of effort. While they occasionally had to coax other students to return to the mat or to settle down, James sometimes needed a reminder to take a break.

Since the Vipassana course James has continued his meditation practice, sitting twice a day on his bunk. He also decided to take his fresh insights and newly available memories of his past and write an autobiography. Although he realizes he may never succeed in getting it published, he feels that meditation has allowed him to discover the value of coming to terms with his past and finding greater peace with his lifetime of incarceration.

Charles Ice

Charles Ice is currently serving a life sentence at St. Clair Correctional Facility, a medium-security prison outside of Birmingham. He was incarcerated at Donaldson in 2002 and attended the first Vipassana course.

Now in his forties, Ice was put up for adoption before he was born. He was told that his mother "had a nervous breakdown" and his biological father was not able to care for him. Adoptive parents raised him, and today he remains in touch with his adoptive mother. His adoptive father died in 2000 while he was at Donaldson. Ice is filled with grief about his father's death and the feeling that his father was disappointed in him. "My father was like a rock. To lose him while I was in prison! I still have not been able to deal with that. I feel I have failed him. And now I worry about my mom, but there is nothing I can do while I am in this place."

Ice traces the roots of the problems that led him to prison to his gentle nature as a small child and his reluctance to fight with other children. "I've lived in a war zone environment all my life. When I was very young, I did not like to fight. There was a bully next door named Ricky. My father made me keep going next door until I could fight back. He wouldn't let me come back onto our porch until I hit Ricky. Through these early experiences my mind was molded to fight."

While in prison Ice became seriously involved with Islam. His reading of the Koran and the regular prayer schedule punctuate his day and help him cope with the losses and stresses of prison. However, for Ice as for others, there is always an underlying sense of suffering and grief. "When you come to prison, you have let everybody down, even yourself. You lose friends, people you thought were your friends. You lose relationships, and everything just crumbles. It is as if you turn into nothing."

When he heard about the Vipassana course at Donaldson, Ice quickly signed up, hoping that it would reduce his misery and sense of failure. "In prison, if you don't move forward, you stand still. Even if I didn't know the right way to grow, I had the desire to find some route to take me forward into growth."

Ice describes the first day of the Vipassana course as "murder on the joints. Day two was easier on the joints, but my knees were something else. It was so hard to sit in one spot. And Bruce kept after me if I stopped working. We called him the 'Dhamma Guard.'" On day three Ice felt himself settling down with a growing ability to work and focus: "From then on, it was like I was purifying myself."

After the Vipassana course Ice made a habit of going to meditate every day with Edward Johnson in his cell. Later, both Ice and Edward were transferred to St. Clair. Away from the other Dhamma Brothers, Edward struggles to keep his daily practice going. Ice, however, has made it a strict part of his routine. Even four years later he manages to maintain his practice, rising early in the morning and meditating before he has to report to his prison job. Although there have been instances when he has resorted to physical fights to stand up for himself, he has also frequently avoided those battles that are so much a part of prison culture.

Edward Johnson

A large man in his thirties, Edward Johnson was sentenced to life for aiding and abetting a triple homicide. He had good reason to question the feasibility of signing up for the Vipassana program. The biggest problem he felt he had to cope with was his own enormous storehouse of anger. He had received so many disciplinary reports he could "paper his cell walls" with them. He was always "scuffling" with corrections officers, going out of his way to subvert their authority over him. "I had a hatred of the administration," he said. He had spent approximately six years in segregation, allowed out of his cell for only 45 minutes each day to walk outside. During those years Edward seethed with anger. The more isolated and restricted he was, the angrier he felt. "I didn't know how to be with myself, how to deal with the monsters inside."

When his six-year-old daughter died of a head injury after falling off a swing, he withdrew further, struggling to maintain the illusion that his daughter was not really dead. He exerted tremendous energy forcing himself to deny her death and to stay constantly preoccupied with everything else so that the reality of her death could not sink in. One of his strategies for coping with prison life was to build a reputation for being tough, someone who was perpetually ready to fight. "I put up a big, bad image, walking tall with my chest out. My street image was 'Edward ain't nobody to fuck with.'" He became active in a gang in the prison and frequently jumped into fights to stand up for his associates.

The roots of Edward's anger, he now realizes, extend back to his childhood resentment of his father's absence from the family and his broken promises to come to Edward's baseball and basketball games. As a child and young man, Edward tried to hold his family together. "I wanted that white picket fence," he says, but instead remembers sitting in a house without heat or electricity. He was the "prodigal son." His mother depended on his stability and help in raising his siblings, but as a young teenager Edward began to drink alcohol. Soon he was missing team practices. At nineteen, while a junior in college on a baseball scholarship, Edward began selling cocaine. After this he was increasingly drawn into criminal activities. When his mother realized he was being caught up in street gangs, she sent him to Chicago to live with a grandmother; however, the lure of the money from drug sales inexorably pulled Edward in deeper and deeper.

After years in solitary confinement, Edward was released back into the general prison population and he began to try to change. He told some of his associates that he didn't want to participate in gang activities anymore. He took an anger management course but felt it just made him suppress his anger. The more he pushed the anger down, the more frightened he became of it. He could sense the buildup of rage inside and didn't know what he would do if he felt provoked. "I was scared. I didn't know when the hell it was all going to come up."

Edward came up to Rick, Jonathan and Bruce at the end of one of the Vipassana orientations and asked them how the meditation would help with his overpowering anger. As they looked into his face, they saw a furrowed, pained and contorted expression. But Edward remembers feeling that "The teachers were freaks. How could they know how to help me? I was just too scared of my anger." As a dominant prison gang leader, he could only hesitantly reveal and confide his fear and doubts about undergoing this experience. Jonathan explained to him how the technique of Vipassana directly addresses anger, not by suppressing it or masking it but, ironically, by allowing it to surface naturally. There we can learn to observe it with an accepting mind. Jonathan assured him that he would find in Vipassana a tool he could use to gradually lessen his anger. He would not be perfect at this practice right away, but he would certainly see change in habitual reactions. Bruce told him he might likely find himself experiencing a lot of anger during the course and should be prepared for that. Reassured, he signed up. On the eve of the course, when he dragged his belongings into the transformed gymnasium and heard the door lock behind him, he was filled with trepidation. Little did Rick, Bruce and Jonathan know that Edward's transformation would be one of the most inspiring to many of the correctional officers at Donaldson.

On the first morning, however, as Edward rose to meditate at the sound of the 4:00 o'clock gong, his doubts only increased. The instruction from the teachers was to focus on the area under the nose as the breath passes in and out of the nostrils. Edward felt this was sheer foolishness. "Man, I already knew how to breathe; I had been breathing all my life." Sitting on his meditation cushion, wrapped in his blanket, Edward struggled to hold still. His legs ached. Then he began to feel hot and itchy. Sweat began rolling off his body. As Edward remembers it, "Even my ankles were sweating." Fearing that he was doing something wrong, he went to Bruce for help. To his amazement, Bruce calmly and confidently explained, "Stay with the breath. You are doing just right."

These instructions from Bruce, and especially the sincere and attentive manner in which they were spoken, made a lasting impression on Edward. Suddenly he was not afraid of his own feelings and physical sensations. Edward felt safe and reassured. This moment is preserved in his memory as a moment of loving, calming responsiveness from an adult. "Bruce will be my partner for life. I love him. He taught me in that moment not to be afraid of myself. And I knew that I was doing something right for a change."

After this encounter, a turning point in his search for relief from his suffering, Edward settled down to the business at hand—learning to sit still and observe himself and his innermost fears and feelings. Over the next two days he doggedly worked on Anapana. "On the first day I was just breathing like I always do. On the second day, sitting on that mat for ten hours, I learned Anapana really well. On the third day I began to feel calm. And then and there, for the first time in my life, I was really ready—ready to deal with Edward Johnson. A lot of guys was afraid to deal with "Big Ed." And now I was ready to take him on, right on that meditation mat."

Relying on his newly honed skills with Anapana and positive feedback from the three guides throughout the long, solitary hours of meditation,

Edward began the practice of Vipassana, directing his awareness throughout his body. He was constantly visited by sensations of heat and feelings
of urgency. At times he had an overpowering need to get away, to run
anywhere and escape from himself. Whenever he retreated to his mattress
in the sleeping area, Bruce or Jonathan were right behind him urging and
coaxing him to get back to his mat. "The process is working. Let the sensations come up. This is what you need to do," was their constant refrain.

Rick, sitting on the teacher's seat directly in front of the men, meditating
and generating an atmosphere of compassion, amazed the students by his
uncanny ability to be immediately aware of their slightest movements or
lapses in meditation practice. Jonathan and Bruce sat just below Rick and
directly in front of the students. Rick would lean forward ever so slightly
and whisper to them when they were needed to escort someone back to
the mat or to give some quiet guidance. Edward remembers feelings of
irritation and even anger on the fourth day when Bruce cajoled him back
to the mat. He had been lying down warding off thoughts of his deceased
daughter. He remembers snapping at him, "I'm coming, man!" Then he
told himself, "Sit down on that mat, Edward, and deal with you." Bruce's
combination of persistence and patience gave Edward the courage to re-
enter the fray going on in his tortured mind.

That night Edward saw his daughter in a dream. She was lying in her
coffin in a white dress, just as he remembered seeing her when he was
escorted from his segregation cell to her funeral. He admits now that he
had tricked himself into believing her eyelids had been fluttering that day
and that she was not really dead. Now, seeing her body in a dream, he arose
from his bed and ran for the door of the gymnasium. "If that door hadn't
been locked, I would have gone flying out of there and down the hall. I
don't even know where I was going." But the door, as always, was locked.
Big E, the corrections officer on duty, gently instructed Edward to go back
to bed. Edward washed his face in the bathroom and paced for a while, not
wanting to have to fully accept his daughter's death. As he remembers, "I
always felt she left me by dying because I left her to go to prison. I never
wanted to face the guilt."

When he went back to bed Edward was again visited by his daughter in
a dream, telling him she was okay. The first person he saw in the morning

was Bruce sounding the meditation gong. When he told Bruce about his dream, not yet knowing how to respond to his fresh realization about his daughter's death, he again received the same reassuring message not to be afraid, that he was doing the right thing by letting the feelings rise to the surface. Buoyed with confidence, Edward felt safe to return to his meditation cushion and sit through the sensations of heat, itching, pain and grief, knowing that this was exactly what he needed to do. By the eighth day of meditation, after 80 hours of sitting and observing his breath and feeling his sensations as they arose and passed away, Edward said, "I was straight. I had learned the process and let the monsters come on up out of me. Now I feel good, even though I am in prison. You can take all the rest of the prison courses and roll them into one, and they don't equal Vipassana. I feel so much better. Now I can sit in my cell for hours, calm and peaceful."

Edward exudes confidence and the resolve to stick to his Vipassana practice and not relapse to his former state—"Big Ed," full of anger and not to be messed with. However, he realizes there are many hurdles ahead if he is to maintain this practice and all that entails. "I've pulled back from my gang activities and now I have to deal with those cats." Recently he was nearby when "Two cats got into a scuffle. When this happens in prison, you don't have to jump in at first. But if your associate can't handle it, you are supposed to help." Following the moral precepts he had committed to when he signed up for Vipassana, Ed is clear that he doesn't intend ever to fight again. So he stood by and watched the fight. "Everybody is looking at me. Is Big Ed going to help or not?" Later, someone came up and called him a "chump," an extremely provocative word in prison, connoting a weakling. To Ed's surprise, no anger welled up in him. As he stood waiting for the familiar wave of anger, he watched his sensations instead. He also realized that, because he himself was quite sure he was not a chump, it didn't matter what anyone else thought or said. Then, "as that cat stood there glaring at me," he found himself smiling and winking at him. Before Vipassana, Ed says, if he had been called a chump, "We would have tore that room up right where we was at. We would have gone down, right on that spot. Trust me. They would have had to call the administration to pull me up off that cat."

As Edward enjoys his freedom from bottled-up rage and his new-found self-confidence, he realizes he may be sorely tested in the future by calls or challenges to stand up and fight. There may be limits to his ability to smile and wink at provocations, and he has been mulling all this over and discussing it with his fellow Vipassana students. He is curious about how he will respond if "someone puts his hands on me." A physical attack, as opposed to a verbal one, "would take it to another level." As Edward ponders this possibility, his first thought is, "I've got to defend myself. No one can just put his hands on me. I don't care about words; I can put words in my hand and crush them up and throw them away. But if someone attacks me, I have got to defend myself. At that point, let's just go in someone's cell and fight." On later reflection Edward begins to construct a possible new solution, one that he would never have entertained before the Vipassana course. "Now that I have changed my ways, if a cat hits me in my face, I've got to swallow that. I'm going to go in my cell and meditate and deal with my sensations. Let the feelings come out. I'm going to use Anapana to deal with myself."

Edward has dropped out of active participation in gang life and the public displays of bravado and machismo inherent in fighting. He eschews his former reputation as "Big Ed." He realizes this dramatic change has left a void in his former place in the gang and raised questions about his strength and manhood. He cried in front of the warden and many of his fellow inmates at the Vipassana graduation. All of this could leave him open to challenge or attack. Yet he maintains that he feels much better, and that he "can breathe again." Unable to cry at his daughter's funeral or at his own trial, he now feels and expresses his emotions.

John Johnson

John Johnson was born in Montgomery, Alabama. His father was in the Air Force and he lived with his mother, father and older brother. He remembers his mother as nurturing and supportive. His parents frequently fought and later divorced. John did poorly in school and dropped out at the age of sixteen. In an effort to cope with his deep insecurities, John experimented with marijuana, LSD and methamphetamine. He became a hippie, moved to San Francisco, and followed the Grateful Dead and the Rolling Stones.

After returning to the South, John's life became increasingly organized around masking his insecurities and supporting his drug addictions. At the age of 26 he was arrested for burglary and spent six years in prison in Florida. Upon release John returned to Alabama where he was twice arrested for first-degree burglary. In 1989 he was convicted as a habitual offender and sentenced to life without parole. Now in his fifties, John has been incarcerated at Donaldson since 1992.

Throughout his life John has struggled to accept a large purple birth-mark spread across the left side of his face. He also has a swollen, disfigured upper lip caused by nerve damage from a childhood injury. As a child he spoke with a speech impediment. "I never felt comfortable because I saw that other children looked different than I did. As I matured in life these bits of baggage that I carried around got larger and larger and larger. I believe that what brought me to prison was an inability to accept myself. I needed to realize that these physical features are not who I really am. Who I really am is inside. But it took me a long time to come to that realization."

For much of his incarceration John has worked to cultivate self-accep-tance and build inner peace. "In prison ignorance prevails and wisdom is often frowned upon. It takes courage to go to a therapy group. It takes courage to lay back on your bed and open up a book that describes prison as a house of healing." Through the Houses of Healing program, John says, "I have learned to forgive myself for the way that I look. By forgiving myself I have been able to feel real remorse for the things that I have done and for the suffering that I have caused other people. By letting go of the past and moving on, I am now able to focus on the present. In our Houses of Healing group discussions we shared our experiences of looking to drugs and sexual escapades to give us freedom, and then finding out that these things pass away and are no longer real. The only thing that is real is what is happening right now."

Although he had been practicing meditation for many years, John was filled with worry and doubt when he first heard about the Vipassana pro-gram. "Why would I want to put in this hard work? I am sitting in prison, which is already hard enough. Why would I want to subject myself to ten days of silence, to remove myself from store privileges, from telephone and the mail, and from chewing tobacco? But I knew that I still needed to understand more about the life that I have in prison. No one had given me any books to read about Vipassana, but I knew that the word meant 'insight.' My imagination was running wild about what this insight was, so I was determined that I was going to find out!"

John entered into the ten-day Vipassana course and embraced the intense battle on the meditation cushion with the hope that it would lead him out of his misery and into a sense of peace about himself. After the course ended he continued the group sittings with his Dhamma Brothers. While living in a three-man cell he arranged to sit a three-day silent retreat by himself, instructing his cellmates about his practice and needs.

John has brought the principles of Vipassana into his daily life in prison. He has maintained his twice-daily individual sittings, his life punctuated by this routine. His letters are imbued with a reverence for the practice of Vipassana, reflected in his learning of its ancient Pali language terms. His correspondence is filled with anecdotes reflecting the application of Vipassana wisdom to the nitty-gritty challenges and stresses of prison life.

Leon Kennedy

Leon Kennedy has been incarcerated for the past eight years on an armed robbery conviction. A slight man in his mid-thirties, he grew up in Birmingham and is the grandson of famed civil rights leader, Reverend Joseph Lowery. Leon struggled with his decision to take the Vipassana course, fearing that it might weaken his great sense of attachment to his young daughter. Like many of the men who wavered in the final moments before the course began, Leon worried about the isolation and the temporary loss of contact with loved ones through phone and mail. Calling his daughter each night at her bedtime reinforced a precious and jealously guarded parental attachment.

Leon also struggled with a different issue. Deborah Marshall told Leon that he would have to take his epilepsy medication during the Vipassana course, even though he felt he no longer had epilepsy. The medication made him feel tired and caused him to experience a loss of equilibrium. "I had to work double hard just to get to some state of normalcy. If I had not had to take the medicine, I still would have gotten many positive things out of Vipassana. But the medicine made me go deeper. It forced me to dig, dig, dig. I had to struggle through every little thing. The medicine filled me with so much anger and resentment, and I had to look at these feelings." When Leon, in a state of medication-induced dizziness, fell off the meditation mat, he heard muffled laughter from the other inmates and felt humiliated. Although young and healthy, he realized he needed to sit on a plastic chair "like an old man" to cope with the drug-induced vertigo. The strong negative feelings arising from the need for a chair, like those from the medicine, became objects of self-observation.

"On the seventh day somebody behind me passed gas really loud and I couldn't stop laughing. Bruce came over and put his hand on my shoulder and whispered, 'Leon, use the breath to get control.' But I couldn't do the Anapana meditation because I was hyperventilating. Later, when everyone came back to the sleeping area, guys were passing gas and there was nothing funny about it to me. So I said to myself, 'What is the difference?' And what I learned is that your stuff will come up and distract you. The mind will distract you and keep you from looking at things for what they really are. What I learned was to be consistent all day long. I made myself do it and do it and do it, staying on top of the technique and examining myself from head to toe and toe to head."

Benjamin "OB" Oryang

Benjamin Oryang, or OB, as he is called, is a tall young man serving a life sentence. Now in his thirties, OB was born in Uganda to a large, wealthy extended family. He is the youngest of nine children. His father also took another wife, a normal practice in Uganda, and had seven children by this marriage. OB's father worked as an engineer for the Ugandan government and also for the World Health Organization.

Throughout OB's childhood, Uganda was ravaged by brutal tribal conflicts and civil war. He has vivid memories of atrocities he witnessed as a boy. One strong memory is of seeing a man, badly beaten and engulfed in flames from having been set afire by a mob, chasing after their car and screaming for help. "After that, I had nightmares. I would see his face as he ran towards my window." There were many times that OB's family sought refuge in the countryside in an effort to escape the violence.

In 1988, when he was sixteen, OB's mother brought her three youngest children, OB and two sisters, to the United States seeking asylum from war-torn Uganda. When they arrived OB found that his education had already prepared him for college here, and returning to high school would be a waste of time. "I was just lounging around waiting for my immigration status to change so I could go to college. I took some computer classes and a nursing course and several other courses at a junior college. I was accepted at Brigham Young University, but I was arrested before I had the opportunity to go there."

OB remembers that, during those early years in the United States, he desperately wanted to be accepted. "I was a stupid kid. I wanted to fit in, to be looked up to by people. I wanted to be accepted in this society here." He began smoking, drinking and carrying a gun, driving around in the countryside with several friends. "I was wild in the partying sense. I had a friend whose mother had a lot of land in the countryside. We used to go out there and do target practice." One night while driving around outside Montgomery, someone in his car shot a gun out the window. "One person got killed and one person got seriously injured. I was convicted of murder and have three life sentences plus 50 years. They are to be served consecutively." The case received a lot of publicity in Alabama. "The media," OB said, "portrayed me as a ruthless, mindless animal from Africa."

During the years of his incarceration at Donaldson, OB established himself as a trustworthy and peaceful member of the prison community. As a runner, he was constantly on the go with errands for the administrative staff. He went on to cultivate advanced skills in mindfulness and conflict resolution. He devoted himself to teaching Houses of Healing classes and has led countless numbers of fellow inmates through this meditation-based program. "These classes have given me peace of mind and lots of tolerance. I stay out of trouble, and not everyone can stay out of trouble in here. It is not because I am obedient but because I have put so much effort into my personal development." Members of the prison staff call for him when there is a threat of violence among inmates. During the Vipassana course he began to realize that he had kept himself busy with people and tasks to avoid slowing down and becoming more aware of his grief.

When he heard the early rumors of Vipassana coming to Donaldson, OB was eager to assist and participate. He remembers that it took three days of observing his breath to begin calming his mind and body. He built a throne of meditation cushions to prop himself up to avoid the pain of sitting. For two days he squirmed and fought his body and busy mind as he attempted to feel his breath. On the third day of Anapana his mind calmed down and he was able to focus on the breath. "I became so aware of everything; I was even aware of my breath in my sleep."

In the middle of the course OB discovered that someone was tying his sandals together whenever he left them outside the meditation area, where no shoes are worn. As the days went by and the prank continued, he became increasingly uneasy. He wondered if he were being ridiculed by a fellow student. He

Shoes outside the meditation area

couldn't push it out of his mind. During the many hours on the meditation cushion, he finally began to meet his bottled-up anger and "the big image" of himself as a "macho man."

On the eighth day he saw the culprit in the act of tying his sandals. "I found myself getting angry, but I couldn't accept this. I am the guy who facilitates anger management groups. My image is that I am well-tempered, in control of everything. I wasn't supposed to feel like this. I was so agitated it took at least fifteen minutes on the mat to begin to calm down. Then I started laughing. I was laughing at the guy who did this. I was laughing at myself for taking it so seriously because I always take things too seriously. Then I realized that maybe I need to learn to relax a little more. Then while I was still laughing, the tears started coming. I have never cried in prison. Initially I didn't know why I was crying, but then I began to realize how miserable and lonely I am. I realize now I have been holding onto grief instead of just letting things go. I have always tried to exercise self-control. With Vipassana, I didn't try to escape from my emotions; I just stayed with them. I was shaking and crying, and tears were rolling down my cheeks. I just stayed there and accepted it for what it was. I know now that that is the reason I couldn't stop crying. But I wasn't embarrassed. And that seems so funny now because ordinarily I would be so embarrassed."

Since that first course OB has maintained his individual practice, encouraged others to keep meditating and, whenever possible, arranged for a group meditation sitting with the Dhamma Brothers.

Omar Rahman

Omar Rahman is in his late forties and has spent the last two decades of his life in prison for robbery and forgery. Over these long years he fought feelings of sadness, guilt and remorse. "I had a lot of negative feelings about what I had done. I didn't like the things I did that led me to come to prison. I didn't like how I felt about myself. For 20 years I have been struggling not to go under because I had read so much about the effects of long-term incarceration on a person. I didn't want to become paralyzed in my ability to exercise my will. After 20 years of trying to overcome what brought me in here, I felt I was becoming atrophied. I just barely had my head above water when Vipassana came to Donaldson."

All Omar's activities in his daily life had been tinged with pervasive dissatisfaction with himself and his past misdeeds. As a leader among the Sunni Muslim inmates at Donaldson, his daily prayers, or *salat*, felt hollow and mechanical. "I know now that I was not giving nearly enough attention and focus to my salat." As a tutor in the prison school program Omar felt "bottled up, like I couldn't express myself," around one of the school instructors. He was overly sensitive to her tone of voice and frequently got his feelings hurt. When she spoke to him, "I couldn't stay in the moment. I would internalize and personalize everything."

With sadness Omar remembers his childhood in Tuscaloosa as one of missed opportunities and a relentless progression down the wrong path. He lived in a house with his mother and four sisters. His divorced father lived across town. "It wasn't middle class, but it was clean and comfortable. There was no violence." Yet Omar felt greatly affected by vivid memories of his mother's sudden withdrawal of love and affection from him when he was four years old. This, coupled with the intensity of her spankings and scoldings, left Omar needing approval from others. "I just can't remember being held by my mother or kissed by my mother or told 'I love you' by my mother, and this affected me into my teens and later on. I gravitated toward people who showed affection to me, and I was always trying to please older females."

An exceptionally bright student, Omar at first sought out the approval of his teachers. Later he felt the need for appreciation and inclusion among his peers. Over the years he withdrew his energy from school and sports and put it into criminal activities. When he tried cocaine, "I got this tremendous sensation and with it this tremendous clinging and intense craving for more. I just thought, 'Hey, this is good.' And for the next six months I began to lose everything I had. I dropped out of college and lost a wonderful woman whom I was engaged to marry."

An accumulation of guilt and despair and a search for self-forgiveness accompanied Omar throughout his long years in prison. As a lifelong avid reader he received succor from books of a spiritual nature. He recently felt stirred by hope when he read *Seat of the Soul* by Gary Zukov. "That book had a profound effect on me and caused me to reach out for more material. I realized then that there is more to me than personality. I learned that we humans are not inherently evil but are inherently good. When Vipassana came along," Omar remembered, "It was the right time for me. I was now ready to go further with myself."

From the beginning Omar knew that he was going to glean all he could from the ten-day course. "Anapana cinched the deal for me from the very first day. I had enough prior experience to know with certainty that this was a very effective way of developing focus and concentration of mind. This caused me to engage myself fully in that process. Every day I experienced greater and greater results." On the fourth day, while receiving Vipassana instructions, Omar felt a sense of freedom. "When we were instructed to go to the top of the head and observe the sensations, I went to a totally different level. I found myself in terrain where I had always wanted to be but never had a map. I found myself in the inner landscape, and at last I had some direction."

That evening Omar felt a tear fall from his eyes. "Something broke. I couldn't stop sobbing. It was one of those deep, deep, deep things. Then I felt myself utter one of those cries where your teeth bare back and your mouth opens. It felt like one of those 'I give, I give, I give' things. I feel it was deeply tied to grief about my mother. I kept having snapshot experiences tied to memories of my mother."

After this intense upwelling of grief and loss associated with the withdrawal of his mother's love, Omar went to talk to Jonathan. "Jonathan told me to back off a bit, work in a more relaxed way and allow integration to happen. I had thought that I had to go through this Navy Seal type thing, so I would go deep enough and get everything out of the experience. After talking to Jonathan I found a more comfortable position, and then I was able to focus more, to engage myself more in the process. The emotion was still there, but it didn't seize me and cause me to sob. The tears continued to flow, and I felt as if I were cleansing myself. I began to observe my pain without reacting to it, and I could see that it was constantly changing. I realized that I could use this in all aspects of my life."

Omar continues to grow and has a new sense of self-worth. After 49 years of "internalizing and personalizing" the reactions of those around him, searching their faces and words to find out if he is lovable, he found love and worth within. The "map of the inner landscape" revealed to him by Vipassana has allowed him to feel more connected to his own truth. The prayers and practice of his Islamic faith are imbued with a fresh new reverence. In his position as school tutor, he no longer feels raw and hurt in his interactions with the instructors. He carries a sense of continuity and stability inside. "I now feel a wholesome attitude in my life. I previously couldn't get there. I couldn't feel it. I didn't have it. Now I feel it. Something has changed in me."

Larry Singletary

Larry Singletary has been incarcerated for more than 20 of his 50-plus years. For many of these years, while serving time in Florida, he says he "fell through a crack in the system." He lived without structure or rehabilitation programs and became complacent about his life, a casualty of long-term institutionalization. With the help of an attorney, Larry's brother had him transferred back to Alabama. Finally Larry shook himself out of his torpor and began to seek structure and treatment inside prison.

At Donaldson, Larry spent a year in the federally funded Road to Recovery therapeutic community for the treatment of drug addictions. He remembers the benefits he felt when his daily life became organized by the structure of the program. At its conclusion he entered the Honor Community, an inmate-led dormitory at Donaldson with a clear daily routine. While living in these in-house restorative communities, Larry began to recover from longstanding depression and low self-esteem. He sought self-help programs such as Houses of Healing, and stress and anger management. The more programs he completed, the better Larry began to feel. When he saw the films Doing Time, Doing Vipassana and Changing from Inside, Larry began to consider the possibility of attending a Vipassana course if the opportunity arose at Donaldson.

A motivating factor for Larry in his search for self-help and treatment programs was his fear of dying in prison. In 1991, at the age of 40, he had had open-heart surgery for severe coronary artery disease. At that time he was told that the surgery would need to be repeated in ten years or less. Larry feels certain that "with the food we get in here and the stress I live under as a prisoner," a second heart operation is now overdue. Since there was very little he could do to advocate for medical care while in prison, his daily life was wracked with fear, anger and the dread of dying inside prison. "I constantly worried about my death, with a lot of hatred toward the medical staff and toward myself for being in prison. I was so afraid of dying in here."

Larry's deep-seated fear of death and his familiarity with inferior medical care has its roots in his mother's sudden death of hereditary coronary heart disease when Larry was 22. "My mom was just a country girl raised up poor, and everybody was her friend. Black or white, it didn't matter; she was a friendly person. She worked hard and tried to raise a family. I couldn't understand why God would let her die. I had a small problem of drinking and doing drugs back then, but she kept me in check about it. After she died I blamed everyone for her passing. I blamed God and my father. I could not accept her death, and I got more and more into drugs."

Larry experienced no last-minute doubts about participating in the Vipassana course. He had waged such a struggle over the years staving off the possibility of his death behind bars that he now craved the quiet and seclusion of the course. Obesity and circulatory problems in his legs make it extremely difficult for him to sit on the floor. A plastic chair was placed nearby for Larry's use when he needed it. He allowed a young man who had a metal plate in one of his legs from a gunshot injury to share the chair. In silence, he and Larry sensitively surveyed each other's need for the chair, and took turns.

Early in the course Larry constantly worried about whether he was following the instructions correctly. "On day four I began to like the whole thing, the meditating, the being alone, the no talking. When there ain't no noise, and you're not talking to nobody, you can go in deeper. And you know, a lot of unpleasant things come up. But if you deal with them to the best of your ability, then the pleasant things start coming. I loved all of it. It was great."

Larry came to terms with his incarceration and his failing health during the course. Acceptance and calm settled like a blanket around his anxiety, protest and denial concerning the possibility of dying in prison. "Now I feel like I can learn to live with a peaceful and happy mind right in this environment. When I die and pass on, I hope I can do it in a dignified, happy way, and that I will leave behind good vibrations." As further confirmation of his increasing level of acceptance, Larry adds, "If my destiny is to be somewhere else, then I'll be somewhere else. But I'm going to be whoever I am, wherever I am at. If I have to be that here in this place, then I am gonna be that here. If I am supposed to get out on parole one day, then I will. If I don't get out, then I'll still be happy and content right here where I am at. It has all got to come from inside me. If I keep it coming out from inside me, then it'll be okay."

Larry has continued to enjoy the benefits of solitary meditation on his bunk. He is pleased that he can sit motionless for a full hour. He says that other inmates refer to the Vipassana students as "the Buddhas." Larry figures that they are envious of the changes they have seen among these men. His friends tell him that he seems more mellow.

He is acutely aware of his new state of mind and the resultant changes in his behavior. "When I first come to prison, it was, like, 'pick out the biggest, baddest dude and go fight him. Then you'll build your reputation and you don't have to fight no more.' But now I realize that's false. All you need to do is just be yourself. Be a human being and treat other people like they are human beings."

Larry has clearly, at least in the short run, received distinct benefits from the Vipassana course. He is continuing his pursuit of inner peace, albeit in a private and solitary manner. He carried a long history of unhappiness and intense inner struggles with his incarceration into the gymnasium at the start of the course. He finished it carrying a sense of peace and resolution back into his daily life.

Rick Smith

Rick Smith is in his late forties and has been incarcerated at Donaldson for the past 25 years. He was convicted of capital murder and has a sentence of life without parole. Rick was born in a small town in Alabama. He dropped out of high school at the age of sixteen and worked in a series of construction jobs and in a chicken processing plant. Always filled with a sense of insecurity about his father's disappearance from his life, Rick easily became involved in drugs and alcohol. He felt increasingly out of control and overwhelmed by his anger and low self-esteem. "The person that I was, was the accumulation of all that woundedness and hurt. I had a good mother, good family. But I had a window of perception that was wounded, which said the world was not treating me right. When you get angry enough, when you get to rage and you get detached, you really don't feel. You've got this place where things are not real." One day Rick walked into a small business and fatally stabbed the woman who was working behind the counter.

For all these years Rick has waged an unending battle to come to terms with what he did that day. He has participated in every available treatment program in prison and sought help from every possible resource. "I have practiced meditation for 22 years. I have a lot more life skills, leadership skills and coping skills now." Along the way Rick discovered a natural ability for leading groups on men's issues, and he has been a teacher in the drug recovery program at Donaldson for many years. His sense of humor and rich story-telling talents have given him great success as a teacher.

Still, Rick felt that he had not gone to the depth of the misery resulting from his crime. On the eve of the Vipassana program he fretted about what he would be facing on the mat. "Because of my remorse I have always wanted to know more about what happened. In fact, my treatment has always centered around me making contact with what I've done. I think one of the things that will come up for me is that my mother and father divorced when I was one year old. I never knew the man. I am hoping Vipassana will help me uncover whole pockets of stuff that I never even got to examine before. I have examined so much about my crime. I don't know if there is more there. But I want to know; I want to make contact with things I never knew before."

During the course Rick confronted his physical and emotional pain. It was so difficult for him to stay still on the mat and not jump and run that he tied himself up with a bed sheet, wrapping it around his legs and back to stabilize himself and prevent shifting and fidgeting. Rick, with his typical humor, referred to this device as his "vipassanator." After the ten days were over, he felt he had met some of his profound pain and survived with a sense of resolution. "I got down to the pain and loneliness under all the anger and hate. You hear that pain and suffering are two different words but, even though you understand it intellectually, it's not until you start to examine yourself inside that you realize that pain is a fact. The pain of my crime is with me daily; I can't get around it. I try to shake it. I've tried to do everything I know to do. When I sit and make contact with it, I find the suffering part has to do with the meaning I attach to my situation, the things I get caught up in. I thought I knew what the word acceptance meant. During those ten days I did a lot of moving. I felt like a mad hatter. But I learned a lot about acceptance and tolerance."

Like many of the Dhamma Brothers, Rick has applied what he leaned from Vipassana. At one point, wrongly accused of drug use and sent to solitary confinement, Rick fashioned his own ten-day Vipassana course. To his surprise, the period of imposed seclusion lasted exactly ten days. The irony of this fact did not escape Rick. Using his daily meditation practice, Rick enriches the programs he teaches with the wisdom he has gained. Although he has health problems and his wife has severe health issues, he has faced these also with equanimity.

Johnny Mack Young

Johnny Mack Young has a sentence of life without parole. He was born in a rural township in Alabama and lived with his parents, an older sister and brother, and a baby sister, Linda. When he was eleven Johnny and his brother got into a fight and accidentally knocked over a gas heater. The house burned down, and Linda was badly burned and later died. In fear of what had happened, Johnny ran away from home.

After living on the streets Johnny was placed in an all-Black reformatory. Desperately unhappy, he frequently ran away, trying to find a way to live on his own. In 1965 he broke into and stole from three different stores to get clothing and food. He was arrested and charged with these three burglaries and given a three-year prison sentence. At the age of 15 Johnny found himself in an adult prison. During this incarceration he got into many fights. "I turned into a hard-core man-child in a violent world where any sign of weakness and you will become a victim." In 1985 Johnny was convicted of murder and sent back to prison. Because of the three prior burglary convictions, he received a sentence of life without parole.

Johnny is in his late fifties and has been incarcerated without a break for more than 20 years. During this time he stopped fighting and trying to run away and decided to make the most of his situation. Recently Johnny has thrown himself into finding ways to heal old wounds and living a positive and peaceful life in prison. He has taken every program available, including Houses of Healing, anger management, stress management and several twelve-step programs. His favorite course was Making Peace with Your Past. Through readings and group discussions he was able to begin to revisit the horrendous details of his childhood and youth, including his sister's death.

Johnny entered the Vipassana program with the same sense of enthusiasm. With support and guidance from the Vipassana guides and the cultivation of new skills in self-awareness and focusing, the course allowed him to delve into his past and explore the multiple traumas, losses and deprivation. Recently he reflected on the impact the Vipassana program has had on the quality of his life. "I needed Vipassana. I've got life without parole and there is a strong possibility I will never get out of here. I was always seeking to escape. My life was in constant turmoil. But when I took the Vipassana course, it changed my thinking. I started seeing ways of being okay with being locked up, being okay with maybe never getting out of here. I can now say that I am okay with my situation spiritually and mentally. I still struggle, but I am not so caught up with whether I am going to get out. I credit that a lot to what I learned in the Vipassana course. This is like freedom, you know. It's like setting me free."

Grady Bankhead

Torrence Barton

Michael Carpenter

Willie Carroll

Wayne Finch

James George

Charles Ice

Edward Johnson

John Johnson

Leon Kennedy

Ben "OB" Oryang

Omar Rahman

Larry Singletary

Rick Smith

Johnny Mack Young

THE LETTERS

From January 2002 to November 2006, Bruce, Jonathan and I received more than 200 letters from the Dhamma Brothers. They were easily identifiable by the words stamped on the back of each envelope, "This correspondence is forwarded from an Alabama State Prison." Each time I received a letter I felt as if a message in a bottle had arrived from a distant shore. Their contents seemed all the more precious and meaningful because of the many barriers between the Dhamma Brothers and the outside world. Even though it was not possible to visit them or even speak on the phone, they were allowed to write.

The letters had an enormous impact on me, each one emphasizing in its own way the contrast between my own comfortable life and the lives of the men—prisoners in a maximum-security prison. As time passed and the letters continued to arrive, I came to realize how important they were as powerful expressions of personal and spiritual wisdom obtained under the most dire and difficult circumstances.

I felt charged with the responsibility of saving each letter. When one arrived I would answer it as quickly as possible. Then I placed each answered letter in a shoebox in my closet. At first, I was not sure what to do with them. As the number of letters grew and their value as a collection became clear, I realized that they needed to be published.

These letters recount remarkable stories with intimate and vivid insights into the Dhamma Brothers' daily struggles, relapses and personal growth as they attempt to construct new ways of living peacefully in their violent and stress-filled world. The letters are presented along with some of the replies the Dhamma Brothers received and some taped interviews. With minor edits for clarity and brevity, the letters and interviews fully reflect the events of each period and bear witness to the profound impact that Vipassana meditation has had on these student inmates. Here, in their own words, are the letters from the Dhamma Brothers.

February 18 – July 8, 2002
Before and After: The First Two Ten-Day Courses

"Never doubt the power of collective consciousness. A couple of years ago I would've thought Vipassana coming to Alabama prisons was only a 'pipe-dream...'"—John Johnson

"I am very happy to have a practice that has opened up my heart to Dhamma. A very great oportunity came to Donaldson facility."—John Johnson

"Seeing the spiritual enchantment on lost souls such as I... Meditating day in and out in seclusion—was something like standing before God telling him everything I'd done, and genuinely being sorry for it. All my past surfaced—the guilt—the shame, the love, the moments of anger."—Willie Carroll

"...along comes inner transformation, even while doing time... along comes seeing the world though a different lens."—John Johnson

"In silence, the mind naturally turns within to observe its own nature."—Rick Smith

"But a bigger prison is the prison of one's behavior patterns. Deep inside, everyone is a prisoner of his unwholesome behavior patterns at the depth of the mind. Without knowing what one is doing, one continues generating some negativity or other: anger, hatred, aversion. By this technique one starts realizing: 'What am I doing? Every time I generate negativity, I am the first victim; I become so

miserable...' Yet out of ignorance you keep making yourself miserable. Now you realize, 'I've got a wonderful technique to come out of this misery.'" —S.N. Goenka

John W. Johnson
February 18, 2002

Dear Bruce,

Greetings from Warrior Lane...

Just think, it was only one month ago when you were part of the process to transform 20 convicts into—pious meditating monks—for ten whole days.

It is still surrealistic when I go to the group meditation. We are a new Vipassana community. We seek to be a warrior of real courage...to be one who is master of his mind.

This prison has the name & history to be known around the state as the "House of Pain." We are new history now.

Let it now be known that Dhamma Warriors here, now offer this declaration:

> Blessed indeed are we who live among those who hate,
> hating no one;
> Amidst those who hate, let us dwell without hatred.
> —*Dhammapada, 197*

Now that the first Vipassana course has come here, here is a major insight I will share with y'all:

Never doubt the power of collective consciousness. A couple of years ago I would have thought Vipassana coming to Alabama prisons was only a "pipe-dream"...

Last week our dearest and very beloved Jenny Phillips came to interview some of us. She brought us many blessings...from y'all. She made mention that we could write you and Jonathan, and ask questions.

I am very grateful to be able to do this, ask questions. Each day brings a flow of questions. Although I have found also that answers seem to flow into my mind. This is really a wild ride. Good, but wild! Some of the questions even seem to lose importance. Here is one that keeps my interest:

Please explain more about the awakening of passion with Vipassana meditation. I know passion is very powerful. It is also an emotion. It also is a reaction word.

Other news for y'all—

This morning we had six to show-up for 5:30 a.m. meditation. Next Sunday Feb. 24th at 5:30 a.m. we will do our first three hour session. Sunday early is a good quiet time for a three-hour.

The 2:30 p.m. meditation group has around six to twelve to show up. Not bad is it? The officers and other prisoners are surprised too.

I think other brothers who do not come to the meditation groups are meditating on their own. Some are I know, they have told me so. We are being gentle with the ones who quit, or going through storms. So far I only know of one who seems to have thunder showers going on.

A newsletter will be a good way to reach out to each one. Maybe you and Jonathan could write half a page for our newsletter? Rick too!

Peace, John Johnson

Bruce Stewart
[undated]

Dear Dhamma Warrior John,

We are delighted about the daily group sittings and especially the three-hour sitting on Sundays. We do have a set of tapes that could be used for a one-day course, but I'm not sure if that could be arranged at Donaldson.

Our ten-day Dhamma journey with y'all was truly an inspiring event. The images of all of you brave warriors working with such dedication and tenacity in the West Gym is now firmly embedded in our consciousness. All of us serving on this course feel so grateful for the opportunity to be part of this remarkable and historic event.

Yes, passion is a very strong and deep sankhara (conditioned mental reaction) for most meditators to deal with; so rest assured all of you are not alone. You ask specifically about "the awakening of passion with Vipassana." Passion, like any other sankhara, is bound to arise as one practices Vipassana...this is natural. We should never feel guilty that passion arises; in fact, we should welcome it and learn how not to indulge it, as this is our opportunity to deal with it at its depth. This is the opportunity to practice Vipassana and come out of the old habit pattern of reacting to and compounding the sankhara of passion. On our Dhamma journey we are all bound to slip and fall down. Goenkaji simply says "Start again,"—no guilt or remorse; pick yourself up and "start again." We should not expect miracles after one ten-day course. The path is very long! Growth in Dhamma is slow and progressive. But it is also subtle, deep and, as you have all discovered, profound and real.

As far as you guys doing your own internal Donaldson Vipassana newsletter, we feel this is a good idea. With this in mind, I will leave you with a very inspiring quote from the Buddha that Goenkaji often repeats to us.

> If wisdom arises in your mind you become humble and modest, as a branch laden with fruit is sure to bow low.

Wishing you and all of your Dhamma brothers peace and real happiness.

With metta, (loving-kindness)
Bruce

John Johnson wrote the following letter one week before the second Vipassana course was held at Donaldson, during the first two weeks of May 2002. Inmate students from the first course were not initially permitted to attend the second course out of concerns of perceived favoritism, but one new student canceled and at the last minute John Johnson was allowed to attend. For the second course, students from the first group had the idea and received permission to meditate together on the other side of the wall of the West Gymnasium, and send *metta* (Loving-kindness) wishes to the new group of meditators.

John W. Johnson
April 25, 2002

Dear Bruce,

Your recent visit brought a welcomed inspiration and was timely. It is very clear that the candidates of the next Vipassana course are truly fortunate for your presence to answer questions of their inquisitive minds.

As we get ready to have new Dhamma Brothers come to our group, we still have a few uncharted aspects of our practice that I think should be addressed.

"Dhamma guidelines for group sittings: Atmosphere before, during, and after sitting." Maybe some suggestions on "Remaining Alert." You know, without futile indulging behavior or idle chats before sitting. It was good you pointed out that we should be maintaining silence during the breaks in our three-hour Sunday sitting. We need this form of suggestions.

This next week I am going to ask for permission to add more time to have for our group daily Vipassana sittings— during the next Vipassana course. Adjustment of East-Hall Therapy Room: 4:30–8:00 a.m., 2:30–4:30 p.m., and 7:00–9:00 p.m.

We could use this time to send metta (wishes of loving-kindness) during the next course in the East Hall Room that is right next to the course meditation hall. For the Dhamma Brothers who want to offer support, we could use this room as a place to meditate, remain silent, or study awareness material. I am willing to make myself available during these hours at the East Hall Therapy Room.

One more week till y'all come again and bring Goenkaji this time…

I offer metta,
John

S.N. Goenka was available to conclude that second course as part of a four-month speaking and teaching tour of the US and Canada. On the morning of May 16, the final day of this second course, Mr. Goenka slowly and silently entered the meditation area and took the teacher's seat on the dais. When the students finished their meditation and opened their eyes, he was there, also opening his eyes after finishing meditating along with them. John Johnson had tears streaming down his face as Mr. Goenka addressed them all. The entire text of Mr. Goenka's talk is provided on page 208. Here are some of the essential ideas he shared with the students who had worked so hard and successfully to complete the course:

> You are now living a better life, more peaceful, more harmonious, not only for your own good, but for the good of so many others, so many others.

> I keep telling people that those who are behind walls are not the only prisoners. Everyone outside this wall is also a prisoner—a prisoner of his own unwholesome behavior patterns of the mind. People have to come out of that—come out of the prison, get liberated.

> I am sure you will be the carriers of the message. You will shine brightly. People will look at you: "Look, what a big change has come, what a big change has come." That will inspire so many suffering people—behind the walls and outside the walls.

> I am sure whatever benefits you have gained during these ten days, if you keep growing, growing in a Dhamma life, you will certainly start shining brightly, becoming a very good example to miserable people around the world.

Edward Johnson
June 13, 2002

Dear Jenny,

You all stay on my mind—in spite of all the mass-confusion that surrounds me every day. You guys have helped change my life tremendously…And I wanna "Thank You" again! I can't seem to stress that enough. I'm just blessed to have had the opportunity to meet a most profound individual, you, and I think of Doc. (Marshall), Rick, Bruce & Jonathan the same way. "God," I did not ever think that I could express myself to people like that. Every time I think of the changes I have made or even hear about them, makes me really realize just how powerful the Technique of Vipassana really is.

I guess you are probably wondering "how is the new class [the second group of Vipassana graduates] doing?" They're practicing what they preach. And you sense the Love & Closeness every time you are in their presence. Now with this last class, people can really look forward to a better attitude in a bunch of men who took the initiative to wanna change their lives. Don't get me wrong Jenny. It is still a challenge for me. Simply because of the high profile I once had as a distraut human being. Everytime I think of how Vipassana has changed my life and taught me how to not bottle things up inside—but to use "Anapana" and deal with it, before it (The Problems) becomes hazardous to me.

Before I end this letter to you, I must comment on seeing "Mr. Goenka" in person. "It surely was a treat!" I don't believe I could ever find the words to use to tell you how impressed I was. I am still in awe!!

I will keep you Posted about my Parole Hearing. They postponed my date again, as of now. Hopefully I will receive another date real soon. My attorney is working day & night trying to get me home. Oh yeah, Dr. Marshall is one person whom I owe a great deal of gratitude to also. She had to get on my case a while back. She thought I was slipping back into the "Gang" atmosphere. She knows I don't lie to her—so I explained to her that I wasn't. She understood and now she isn't mad with me anymore. I saw her last Friday & she actually gave me a thumbs up. That meant a lot to me. I'm a grateful person. I will never let you guys down…nor myself for that fact.

Sincerely,
Edward Johnson

Benjamin Oryang
June 26, 2002

Dear Jenny,

This evening I had some fun with a few of my dhamma
brothers. During the sitting at about 3:00 p.m., something very
heavy and cold landed on my arm. I opened my eyes in surprise, and got even more surprised to discover that the culprit
was a regular looking fly. It continued to crawl across my
bald head, face and arms through the sitting, and I was totally
amazed at how heavy it seemed to be. To myself, I named the
different body sensations I was experiencing at the time: heat
sensations, sound sensations, fly sensations (very new to me)
and several more. Immediately after the sitting, everyone
started complaining, at the same time, about the fly: There was
actually only one fly in the group room. As it turns out one fly
had terrorized eight hardened prisoners for a whole hour. Even
though we didn't kill it, we spoke of several things which could
be done to it. We then started wondering about how a fly lands
on a ceiling. Have you ever looked up on a ceiling and seen a fly
perched upside down? How did it land there? Did it fly upside
down in order to get there?

We discussed fly issues for over ten minutes. Afterwards,
we began to question our own states of mind for wondering so
much and taking the fly so seriously. We still couldn't figure
out how flies land on ceilings.

With the fly and our craziness aside, things here are continuing about as would be expected. And even though the average number of Vipassana meditators coming to each sitting is
down to five or six, all the guys (both old and new students) are
very supportive of each other. I have tried not to take any lead
role concerning the sittings, hoping that this would encourage the guys to get more involved, but it is now time I took
some action to try and get all my dhamma brothers actively
involved with the group sittings, etc. Of course, you were right
to think it is difficult to maintain the practice without some

outside help. There are quite a few things which Dr. Marshall is incapable of doing in her capacity as a staff psychologist here. Actually, it is left up to us guys to make things happen; you guys have all done your parts to the fullest.

By the way, the Houses of Healing class and all the other groups are going on pretty well. This keeps me so busy, but helps to pass the time constructively.

Your friend,
OB

Interview with Benjamin Oryang (OB)

Jenny: Well, OB, you said that you were trying to figure out what had really changed since Vipassana. Has anything changed, and if so, what?

Yes, a lot has changed. And the thing that comes most clear to me is that sometimes it seems as though everything is okay. I don't panic, or I don't rush to judgment like I used to before. I was giving the example of the shift officer people. Trying to get them to announce for [meditation] groups, sometimes it's real difficult here. There's all this stuff going on, and they don't want to announce for [the] group. They might not want to open the door so that we can have access to the room. I think I'm a lot more patient now. I think I don't even hold resentment towards them when they do this; before I think I did. Before, I might let it bother me a little bit. I might get a little mad at them or something, but I haven't got mad at them this time. You know, it's all okay. I've been going with the kind of attitude, like, well, if we don't get it done now, might be later—and it doesn't matter—I don't get upset or anything. I notice that that's a big, big change. If I just view things with equanimity, then I don't think I can go wrong.

What were those tears about on the tenth day [of the Vipassana course]?

I felt as though I'd never really been happy before in my life. But on that day, I was, you know; I actually felt happy. I was there, I was happy, in prison with a life sentence, really I've got a few life sentences, but it's called a life sentence—I don't know what's going to happen with my life or anything, but I was so happy.

Well, what is Vipassana and how does it change people?

It is one thing to know something intellectually. And there's so many intellectuals here and in the world out there but especially here—everybody's an intellectual. I probably thought I was an intellectual before Vipassana. Sometimes I sit and wonder how that could be possible that I felt the way I did during those arduous ten days. Because I can sit down now, I feel the sensations, the body sensations, and I go through a sitting doing Vipassana. I was wondering how it was possible following all the precepts we're supposed to be following, following all the guidelines that our teacher has asked us to follow and whatnot, you know; and then we go through all this and that helps so much for the mind to actually calm down and then there's none of the outside stuff to worry about. Everything is taken care of, you know, so you have all the time to put your attention to working on you, to doing the work you're supposed to do on the mat, you know. One is able to gain so much, so much, and it's not intellectual at all. You know, it's all experiential. When I sit down now and see somebody who was there—one of the guys who was there with me or somebody who has attended a Vipassana course before—I look at them as a different kind of person. I don't look at them as just an intellectual. You know there's something different about them because they've experienced that thing that they've gone through, that experience, you know. They have that wisdom, they have pañña (wisdom), you know, they have the experiential wisdom. It's not just intellectual stuff anymore. So it's very different. It's a big difference.

I guess you could say everybody needs Vipassana, but how do you feel about the appropriateness of it for prisons? Do people need this in prison?

I think they do. I think it should be in every prison in the United States. I think every prison should give the opportunity for a Vipassana course, so the guys could attend. I think they should.

Are there any other programs that you've come upon in prison that gets to the same things that Vipassana does?

No. There are a lot of programs that might help to prepare one for Vipassana, like Houses of Healing for one, but I don't think anything quite gets to that level. I don't think it does.

And you need to get to that level, you think?

I think it's necessary. I think everybody should at some point in their life. I think it would be a big turning point for a lot of people who are in prison, because most guys in prison are intellectuals. They know everything—they know everything about everything, and it's hard to tell them anything. It's hard for them to accept things that they're told. This is what they take to be somebody else's intellect, 'cuz most of us in prison, most of us prisoners are selfish. We're very selfish and the environment breeds that.

Bruce Stewart
July 1, 2002

To my dear Donaldson Dhamma brothers:

I am writing from Shelburne after leaving S.N. Goenka's Meditation Now tour in San Diego. I'm happy to report that the tour is going well, that all of Goenkaji's public talks are well attended and, like yourselves, old students are delighted to meet and meditate (mostly for the first time) with Goenkaji in one-day courses at each location.

Many of your unknown Dhamma brothers and sisters have taken such interest in your efforts and success in Dhamma. When we describe how diligently you all worked and correspondingly just how much you benefited, people are so moved and inspired.

Dr. Marshall informs me that the numbers at the daily group sitting are swelling. This is good news! Remember that Vipassana only works when you practice it. Otherwise Vipassana just becomes a wonderful memory…"My course was so good, the discourses were great, the technique is great and, oh, the food was unbelievable, etc." To really get the benefits of Dhamma one has to practice it. One hour in the morning and evening is essential. One has to keep cultivating the deep understanding of impermanence—anicca, anicca, anicca—to come out of the old negative habit patterns of blindly reacting with craving for the pleasant and aversion for the unpleasant.

Often a new student becomes discouraged after their first course because they cannot develop the concentration (samadhi) to feel sensations the same as they did during the course. This is natural, as one cannot expect to have the same deep experience as when one is making continuous efforts during a ten-day course. It is so important not to get frustrated and give up. Keep making efforts. Work more with anapana (observing the breath), then move quickly through the body for a while (even if you do not feel sensations everywhere), and change the way you work so you do not become bored. Even if your meditation is not going well, never get frustrated and increase the *sankhara* (conditioned mental reaction) of frustration by reacting with negativity. Remember, the key is your equanimity: "This will also change." Also be aware of the trap of "playing the game of sensations." It does not matter what kind of sensations you experience; it is your equanimity that counts. This, and this alone, will liberate you from the bondage of misery and suffering.

As you all know, the entire teaching is sila (morality), samadhi (concentration) and pañña (experiential wisdom). Cultivating and developing a strong base of morality is critical to your successful growth in Dhamma. Hence the five precepts play a critical role in gaining mastery over the mind. With a strong and focused mind, one can then develop experiential wisdom from knowing the changing nature of this mind/body phenomenon that we call "I, me, mine." We do this by observing the ever-changing sensations in the body. This is the deepest level of the mind and is where all our suffering originates.

Your efforts and success are an inspiration to many. Jonathan, Rick and I sincerely wish you success in your efforts. We feel fortunate to have had the opportunity to meet and work with you.

Bruce

Interview with Leon Kennedy

Jenny: What made you decide to do the program?

My close friends, Troy and OB, who also participated in the course. They were trying to explain to me [that I'm] not going to lose love for [my daughter] or anything, and I told them that I understand that but I don't want not to be attached to her. I want to be attached 'cuz I'd made myself so dependent upon that—it was a part of my sanity, a part of my everyday walk of life—that little girl. And she doesn't know it, she doesn't understand it. She's just, you know, she's just who she is, and I'm just so attached to my daughter, my child, my beautiful baby girl.

Did Vipassana change your love for your daughter?

Yes, it did. It changed it in the sense of it being enhanced by the overall view of what love really is. I wasn't loving her—I was selfish—I was loving me. I was utilizing my love for her to comfort me, although I was showing her that I love her and telling her. But that's not what love is, that was not complete love for her.

Leon, can you say something about the technique and how you felt it working in you as the love changed?

As the love changed, I had heard the term "liberated" used throughout these days, and by the fifth day I wanted to break my vow of silence to go and grab my friend OB and tell him, "Hey, I am liberated." I wanted to while we were in the hall because the feeling was so overwhelming. I knew what love was, and I cried and I cried.

What were you liberated from?

I felt like I let go of what I thought love was. And it wasn't just with my daughter; it was with my wife, my mom, my sons, my father. You know you're rooted with these people. This is what you base your life on and it answers so many other questions in life. It's a master key to so many doors of insight, and I'm just loving them now. I was like, now you love 'em. And I love me now. Yeah.

Can you give an example, Leon, of a situation that you look at differently now?

So many. Department of Corrections—everyday we have to go and ask the shift officers to announce for the classes that we teach, and everyday they give us a nasty, nasty hard time. All we're asking them to do is "Will you please announce for 'blah, blah'?" and they give us such a hard . . . They say nasty things to us. They make it like you are such a nuisance or, like, "Why were you born?" type thing, and it doesn't affect me. I smile at 'em and wait till they announce it and tell them thank you very much, and I leave without any negativity or any holding onto any negative or snickering thoughts about 'em.

What might have happened before Vipassana?

Before, I would show them that face, you know, that thank-you-very-much face, and when I leave I take that with me. I take that negative stuff with me and be mumbling about it all the way down the hall, like, "God, man, you know, what's wrong with these people?" Now, it doesn't even matter. It doesn't even matter. That's not like the main thing I got out of Vipassana— it's just a love thing is what I really got.

That's the main thing?

That's the main thing. Everything is a love thing. No matter what. You got to love 'em, 'cuz if you don't love 'em you're not being true to yourself and [if] you love yourself, you know, it's like you've got to meet everybody on an equal level. Equal level—everybody. When I see anybody, it's like I get happy. I don't know 'em, and I've got attitude like, hey, here's—ah, I don't even know that person but here they are, you know—and we speak or what have you. My entire life has changed, my wife, my relationship with her. It has enhanced all of my relationships, family and friends. But my wife, you know, she's curious about it. She wants to take a course. My daughter, my daughter—I can't even explain what it's done with me and my daughter because we have a—all fathers think they have a special bond with their daughter, but my mom, my wife, everybody says that my child and I have, like, this super bond. It's grown. She's like—there's so much more now than what I thought, what I saw on the surface level. I'm just so fortunate to be able to come here and take that course. It's amazing. I had to come to prison in order to be free, and it's stupid, I guess, but it happened.

What was it like for you to have these three men come in and lock down in prison with you and really, really take care of you, clean your toilets, make sure you're okay, really very lovingly take care of you?

It was a humbling experience. They had so much humility, they didn't mind. They actually applied and asserted themselves strictly for that. "This is what we are here for," and it made it so easy to say, "Hey, I'm hurt," you know. It created atmosphere, and the egos didn't get in the way. I can tell you, I can cry in front of 'em. Hey, this guy's cleaning up after me, this guy is preparing my food, this guy is doing all this stuff so I can share with him my innermost pain and thoughts and dumb questions and stuff like that. It was amazing. I love them forever. They will always be special to me. They were like ground zero, you know?

Like what?

Ground zero: They were on the front lines with us—like, hey, take your medicine, ring the bell, showers, the food, walk with you outside. They're sleeping here in this prison with us because—and I'm quite sure they were discussing us or like, "Hey, we're in prison with them. Look what they're doing." Well I was looking at what they were doing too. They're in prison, man, with us. They are staying here. They have lives too; they have wives, jobs and children. It was amazing. It created so much—I can't think of the proper word for it—so much gratitude. Even to the extent of the cooks—anybody who was helping—it made everything so much more special, to prepare our food, to cook it. We didn't spend one red cent. People we don't even know were supporting us as an institution for this type of practice. So it was a very grateful feeling.

What happened when you went back into population again, and the Vipassana course site in the gym was taken apart and everybody left?

Everybody left. OB and I were the last ones. To take down—you know, taking everything down—it was sad. Yeah, we had to break it down; yeah, it was rough. And even rougher than that—that was sad, that was truly sad—but even rougher than that was going back out to the general inmate population. All the noise, all these vibrations, everything was so loud. It was so loud. You know, the screaming, the normalcy of everyday prison life was—it took me about a week to filtrate back into the swing of things. That was why the follow-up, the meditation, the 5:30 a.m. and the 2:30 p.m. sitting that we still do now, was so important. It was so important because we could sit down and get that atmosphere back. The same atmosphere that we had in the gym would be in that room amongst us. That energy was in us, and we can also talk about our experiences in a safe environment again. So I guess you can equate the safety of the environment, the atmosphere in the gym, with the people; it has a lot to do with the people as well.

Can you say anything about the mistakes or things that brought you into this place?

Bank robbery. I weighed out my consequences. I weighed out even that I might leave my daughter. Had I done Vipassana first that wouldn't have been a reality because I wouldn't have been deluded by my mind. I'd have been seeing things for what they really are. I wouldn't have loved the way I thought love was. Had I learned how to love, even as a ten-year-old boy, things would have been different. I keep referring back to this love thing. It's just so important to the universe, you know. It expands more than just an emotion—it's a way of life. How we interact with each other and see each other. So that's what I've learned most out of Vipassana, something I cherish, and I'm going to teach to my kids and anyone that will have an open mind. We all need to love each other more.

July 9, 2002
Shut Down: Courses and Group Sitting Privileges

> *"Really, I think that the administration would rather see 'chaos with vain superstition,' because this is familiar and does not shake their false zone of comfort."* —John Johnson

> *"Even though it is good to have group sittings, each one of us has still got to develop his own practice. Further, things are bound to change; nothing is permanent."* —OB Oryang

> *"So many of our Dhamma brothers are hanging tough."*
> —Rick Smith

"Speaking of upheavals we could use a cultural one in this State. This state is so hide-bound to a narcissistic view of reality and human affairs.... We still march to the palpitations of past prides and prejudices here. Progress here is a backward looking affair and change is a slow-moving train that never seems to stay moving long enough to get anywhere." —Omar Rahman

No official explanation was ever given. On July 9, 2002, word came that the Department of Corrections had shut down the Vipassana program. It became clear that at least one individual in power had found the fact that the Vipassana courses were based on the teachings of the Buddha too threatening in a fundamental religious sense, even though the teachings are carefully presented in the same strictly universal, nonsectarian way that the Buddha originally gave them. So, without warning, restrictions were suddenly put into place in an effort to revert to the status quo. The Dhamma Brothers were no longer allowed to meet together and meditate, and more courses could not be organized and given. However, although this represented a real setback, Dhamma was already out of the bag.

Benjamin Oryang
July 14, 2002

Dear Jenny,

Thanks for writing. We here are continuing to survive, even though we have been presented with a new challenge.

On Tuesday the 9th (last Tuesday) we were informed that there will be no more Vipassana activities at Donaldson Prison. This cancellation included not only the ten-day courses, but also the daily sittings which we had in the group-room. Even after raising all the expected questions about this action, we have not been given any explanation or reason for the cancellations. Further, we are not expecting any to be given—and have all agreed to just sit with things as they are for now. But in light of the fact that none of the other programs here have been cancelled, the urge to take some kind of legal action has been smouldering right beneath the surface. The Vipassana meditators are handling the situation with a very admirable calm but, surprisingly, many of the other prisoners and several staff members (including COs with rank) are the ones who are calling for and actively considering taking some action.

Otherwise, I, personally, am continuing to sit in my cell. Even if I miss the air which we had created in the group-room and find it more of a challenge to meditate in my cell, I am determined to continue the practice. Also, whenever I run across any of my Dhamma brothers, I feel obliged to give them some encouragement towards the continuation of practice; I remind them that even though it is good to have group sittings, each one of us has still got to develop his own practice. Further, things are bound to change; nothing is permanent.

On the other front, I now have a lawyer to represent me for purposes of parole. This came as a very good development, as it would have been almost impossible for me to satisfactorily represent myself before the Board of Pardons and Parole. With the lawyer, I now have to piece together a support group and also do some further investigations to determine exactly how to present myself before the Parole Board.

My mother is excited about the lawyer, but she has had a rough week due to severe swelling in her legs. Otherwise she is hanging in there and continuing to do all she can to help me. I love her so much.

Your friend,
OB

John W. Johnson
July 21, 2002

Dear Bruce,

Greetings to each of y'all—our precious Dhamma family. Within this mailing you will find a bookmark I made around three years ago. It is my wish for you to have it.

The items contained therein were collected at different times . . . from many different areas of the yard grounds at Donaldson. During my duties as a maintenance worker my job took me throughout many areas of this compound. As a meditator these items were part of the observations that sprang up to my attention. It was an awakening process to the natural beauty of nature that surrounded one even in a prison setting. It was the start for me seeking a cultivation of my meditation practice.

Over the years this book mark has been an aide to me. It has brought me to my simple awareness of nature. It has helped me mark a point of concentration . . . to the pages of some of the wonderful books I read over the years. Most of these books were written insights of people of the past who were on a path of awakening. These insights of people I read about, and their experiences, became a part of my consciousness. Of course these mental images were only a process obtained in my imagination. I have since come to understand it was like the saying, "counting the sheep of another's herd."

Now that I have a practice that offers a direct path to awakening myself and my other Dhamma brothers…[We] are realizing insight from our own experiential level of consciousness. We are greatly appreciative. We acknowledge your compassion.

The guidance offered by Goenkaji during the May visit still resonates. The following are a few areas of my practice:

I meditate at least twice a day. Since our loss of space to serve as Dhamma meditation hall, I practice at my living area. Sometimes three to four times a day. Going deep too.

As a community service I am servicing the ice machines. I no longer work maintenance, but saw a need to insure the compound had plenty of ice during the hot summer months. Ice brings happiness. It has been a rough experience.

I no longer support the prison contraband market. [This includes] food from the chow hall and any other stolen items from different departments, such as ink pens, soap, etc.

Last week I had an interesting dream about being around people I had never been around before. We meditated together.

Later I held my arms out and these people joined in with me shoulder to shoulder with our arms outstretched. I felt a sense of compassion. I think it was a metta experience in my dream stage of sleep. There were men and women in this sweet dream. I awoke very happy.

So this is an update. I guess some of the other Dhamma brothers here are keeping their practice going. I do not know for sure.

Do know that I will continue. "The Noble Eightfold Path: The Way to the End of Suffering," the book by Bhikkhu Bodhi, has been very helpful.

Your letter in the newsletter made everyone come together for a while. This was good. Also, your letter to us later was handed out on the day we lost the privilege to meditate at a central location. Your compassion and insight helped us through a rough time. I want you to know this.

John

Bruce Stewart
August 18, 2002

Dear John:

It is such a great thrill for us to know that you have benefited so much from Dhamma. Yes, Goenkaji's visit was truly remarkable in so many ways, and I'm happy to hear that it continues to give you strength and inspiration. Goenkaji left for Europe two weeks ago. It is conservatively estimated that he reached forty thousand people through the public talks during his Canadian and U.S. tour. Several locations packed halls well over a thousand. He was extremely happy with the success of this unique Dhamma mission.

While Goenkaji was here we formed a new "Corrections Trust" [Vipassana Prison Trust] specifically to raise funds for ten-day courses in jails and prisons in North America. It will also focus on outreach to other institutions.

As a response to your notes on your practice:

1. I'm pleased you continue to sit at least twice a day and very happy that it may be as much as three or four times. Sit as much as you are able; it will give you great strength.

2. Any community service you can do is wonderful. Doing humble and selfless service will do much to fulfill your paramis (noble qualities). I was just reading about Sariputta, the chief disciple of the Buddha, who was known for doing simple and often mundane service for others. This all helps break the attachment to the notion of "I, me, mine."

3. It is wonderful that you no longer support prison contraband. As you meditate more, your understanding of *sila* (morality) becomes deeper, and naturally some inappropriate actions just fall away.

4. Your description of your dream was moving. Yes, *metta* (loving-kindness) will fill you in different ways as you both give and receive it.

5. If you have the chance, please encourage your Dhamma brothers to keep up their practice. As I have said in the past, Dhamma only works when you practice it; otherwise it is just a good memory. Incrementally and according to one's past parami, the Path will reveal itself. Have no doubt!

Of course we are all disappointed you have lost the right to hold your group sittings. I know how much this has meant to you all. I was encouraged and impressed that you did not express any negativity about this situation. I encourage you all to stay calm, trust in Dhamma and send metta to all those involved in this unfortunate decision. Maybe the time will ripen when you can politely ask to have these sessions back again.

While Goenkaji was here recently at the Vipassana Meditation Center in Shelburne, we had a special returning students program which was attended by over 300 students. Jenny came and we showed some of the rough film footage that was shot at Donaldson. The response was overwhelmingly positive. People were truly amazed and inspired by the heartfelt, insightful and articulate manner in which you all expressed yourselves. The Dhamma brothers at Donaldson have done a wonderful service and stand as an inspiration to many. Some may recognize the irony of men, locked away in a maximum-security prison, inspiring others to live wholesome and Dhamma lives. But this is a fact!

Bruce

James George
August 14, 2002

Greetings my Dhamma Sister,

Ms. Johnson told me this morning that she had talked with you over the weekend and you asked about all of us. Well, for the most part we are doing fine, only concerned that we are no longer allowed to practice our meditation as a group. Have you heard anything more on why the administration stopped it? Of course some of us continue to practice at our living area, so all is not lost.

I have a question concerning how we sit. I talked with several of the guys in the program who went through Vipassana about sitting for ten hours one night and they all would like to do it. However, what I need to know is, will this in any way jeopardize the future of Vipassana courses being offered here at Donaldson? None of us want to do anything that might create a problem later down the road for you guys coming back. There has been a very definite impact, even with correctional officers, and it's something that certainly needs to be continued. I firmly believe the visit from Goenkaji had a profound effect on many people here and I'm not talking about only inmates.

Jenny, speaking from personal experience, I must say that Vipassana had the most profound effect I have ever witnessed on a group of inmates. Although it didn't effect all the way it did some of the others and myself, it did have some kind of effect on everyone who took it. The changes I've noticed within myself have made a remarkable difference in the way I view things (equanimity). I'm able to deal with situations more calmly than before because now I can see everything in a better perspective. Wouldn't it be wonderful if it were mandatory that all prison personnel attend a Vipassana course?

Your Dhamma Brother,
James George

Benjamin Oryang
August 24, 2002

Dear Jenny,

On the Donaldson front, there is nothing new to report. We still have not been given any explanation or reason for the administration's expulsion of all Vipassana activities over here. On September the 9th it will be two months since we were informed of the action. On that date, I plan to request an interview with the warden in [light] of his position as over-seer of this prison. I intend to inquire as to why all Vipassana activities were expelled, and find out if there is anything that we prisoners can or need to do in order to have the said activities reinstated. I don't know where my inquiry will lead, or what will come of it, but it would be interesting to know exactly what is going on; maybe then I could decide what course of action to take next, if feasible. I will keep you informed of any developments.

OB

Benjamin Oryang
Sept. 21, 2002

Dear Jenny,

With the expulsion of the Vipassana group sittings now pushing towards its third month, the Dhamma community at Donaldson is feeling many of the expected results. I wish I could say that my personal practice hadn't been affected, but that would be running far from the truth.

In looking at this situation from a more optimistic angle, I think it is correct to say that we are actually gaining experiential wisdom on the benefits of group sittings. Twisted thinking? And even though it would be nice to sit with the group again, it is still true that it is the practice—not the group practice—which is most important. So even though there still aren't any new developments with regards to the reinstatement of the group sittings, the continuation of practice needs no special conditions and, thus, can only be stopped by the individual.

Metta,
OB

John W. Johnson
September 29, 2002

Dear Jenny,

Well life is truly different since the second Vipassana [course]. I started reading all I could get my hands on, with the practice of Buddha—"The Enlightened One."

The Theravada practice is just right for a convict. It is so direct. I see this practice as a great opportunity to explore while doing time. "If not now . . . when?" makes good sense. Over the years past I wasted too much time. As the saying goes . . . "what good does it do studying the scriptures of ancient teaching and then just counting the sheep of another's persons herd." One must practice.

As you know, Jenny, this is not an easy practice for one who is in prison, or out. I will say it is wild observing the arising of conditional states. It is easier to see it with other people still, although I have become more aware of what is happening within me too.

Everything is so much more real. This is an interesting experience. Boredom is an experience of the past. No longer bored.

It is, though, difficult seeing people who suffer, and they can not understand the cause they bring upon their own experience. This is very true with family members who I love deeply and have a long history with.

Peace, *John*

James George
November 1, 2002

Dear Bruce,

I received your letter and was truly inspired by it. I also shared your letter with Ms. Johnson and Mr. Blackmon [in the drug treatment program].

Bruce, when we were first informed by Dr. Marshall that we could no longer meet for group sittings, there were many who questioned the validity of such a decision. Of course Dr. Marshall cautioned all of us about becoming negative and encouraged us to remain calm and be patient.

Unfortunately many have since stopped practicing, and this saddens me. Several who were so enthusiastic in the beginning seem to have drifted away from practicing. However, I know that all I can do is continue to work toward my personal enlightenment, allowing each to decide for himself. In this respect it is just like treatment; one must concentrate on working his personal program and not dwell on what another does.

Personally, Bruce, I find such peace in sitting daily. Occasionally I sit for two hours in the morning and, as difficult as it may be to believe, the second hour is always better than the first. With this in mind I have decided to do six hours this Sunday. I plan to begin at 10:00 p.m., take a 15 to 20 minute break between each hour, take an hour out for breakfast and finish up by 6:00 a.m. I'll let you know how it turns out.

It is my fondest hope that you all are allowed to bring Vipassana back into Donaldson. It can make such a difference in the collective minds of men here, which in turn could let society as a whole acknowledge that people can and do change.

Metta, *James*

July 28, 2002
Dhamma Brother Transferred

"Non-harming communication takes skill, especially in a hostile environment where people are in such emotional state of suffering."—Leon Kennedy

"The inconsistent nature of the mind, mixed with the power of perception-delusions are always near and waiting to taint our inner peace."—John Johnson

"The power of doing Vipassana in prison—a perfect setting. It is a place where so many people experience appearance of all the aggregates—sorrow, lamentation, distress, despair."—John Johnson

Edward Johnson
July 28, 2002

Hello Jenny,

I'm going to make this letter short & to the point. I have been transferred to another camp. It's really a blessing. Therefore I choose not to complain about it.

There is so much that is going through my head right now—as I sit in the dorm of "Kilby." I don't know how long I'm gonna be here. Hopefully it won't be long. My next camp will probably be Atmore. It is a lower Level 4 camp. Yes Jenny, "a much better facilitated camp." Now my next move will be home. I haven't received another parole date yet. But my attorney said it will be in November. So make sure you keep me in your prayers.

Ever since coming into the Vipassana technique, I have really met some cool & beautiful people. The day that I let go of my past and allowed the practice of Dhamma to take its course—was the day I found peace from within. After learning how to develop (master) awareness and equanimity towards sensations, I can actually see a much brighter future.

Edward

Interview with Edward Johnson

Jenny: What were you taught in Anger Management?

Push it down, walk around, walk away, you know. But . . . .

And you don't think you should walk away when you're angry, turn the other cheek? What do you think you should do?

Yes. Well, in Anger Management it teaches you to just say "Okay, if he hits you, don't hit him back." Turn and walk away. But with what I've learned now—with the Vipassana—you know, somebody piss you off, just start to [do] my respiration [anapana] and you know, cool—laugh and smile and you still be happy. And I feel much better about that. I never ran [into] a course like this before. And it's all been, you know, say real good. Prison is not rehabilitating a man just with the courses that they throwing at you. It's just officers that they try and put at you, you know. Officers make you more angry. They come here with problems.

Yeah, and you don't think [prison] courses rehabilitate you?

Well, not the courses that they having now, but this Vipassana—that's rehabilitation. You soul search in that.

What's the difference—can you really identify it—between the Anger Management course and the Vipassana course?

Anger Management, like I said, was just, you know, they tell me [to] suppress it. With Vipassana, they let, you know— you got [to] let the sensations come up out and make you feel better about yourself. Deal with it what you trying to hide. You know, no hiding; let it come up.

Edward, tell me something about Vipassana—I mean the first three days of your sitting.

I was tripping. I was! The first three days I was tripping.

What does that mean?

Like when they teach you how to breathe and all this, I started getting hot and itching and my head starting getting hot, and I was, like, what the hell's going on?

Edward Johnson
September 16, 2002

Dear Jenny,

Jenny, things here with me is sort of hectic. I've been going through some tough times since leaving all the love & support of my Dhamma family at Donaldson. True enough it's been hard lately...especially trying to adjust from a max camp after a lot of years, to a lower level camp. My patience are definitely being tested. Then, not only the aggravation of dealing with the administration—but also dealing with a bunch of guys who is coming to prison for the first time...with no morals, self-respect, or values instilled in them. It's tough being here!! Last but not least, I am still in limbo about my parole. Now thats frustrating. I wished I could close my eyes, wake up and all this will be behind me.

Now Jenny, don't get me wrong, I'm not giving up. I have come too far to give up now. I am merely stressing & venting to a special friend. So please don't worry. I will be okay...some-how, someway.

I know you are asking yourself, "Am I still meditating?" I'm not going to lie to you either. The answer is "Yes & No." I have been meditating. Sometimes with focus and sometimes with-out. And the technique doesn't work unless you are focused. Like the focus I had tonight. It was lovely. I felt at peace.

I have made a tremendous change in my life. And basically it is due to you all…starting with Doc. She inspired me like no other. Then I met you, Rick, Jonathan & Bruce. I refuse to let myself to slip back into my past. It held me back from progressing after so many years, I have been a fighter all my life. Therefore I refuse to stop fighting now. It's a struggle. However, it is a struggle that will only make me more stronger. Because I will never give up.

Love.

(Your friend 4-Life)

Edward

Bruce Stewart
October 22, 2002

Dear Edward,

Just yesterday Jonathan and I were doing a presentation at a local jail where we were showing the ten-minute film clip Jenny made. There you were in the film describing your Vipassana experience and expressing your heartfelt feeling of gratitude for the Dhamma.

Edward, I strongly encourage you to keep up your practice. From what I gather you are managing to do this, but it must be difficult for you. While it is ideal to sit together in a group, it is not absolutely necessary. Remember, the Dhamma is inside! No one can take this away from you. As the Buddha says, "You have to make an island unto yourself.'

Always remember, even in the toughest of times, everything is changing. The apparent solidity of storms and prison life melodrama are also changing—nothing is permanent—it will all pass away. With constant practice the illusion of "I, me mine" slowly gets shattered by the deep understanding and wisdom of *anicca* (impermanence).

This is all based solely on one's own experience. This is the beauty and power of Dhamma—there is no blind belief just because the Buddha or your teacher says so. It is based on your own experience, bhavana-maya pañña (experiential wisdom). It is a "law of nature," pure and simple.

Bruce

Edward Johnson
October 30, 2002

Dear Bruce,

Bruce I am basically maintaining. I enjoyed reading the [transcript] of Mr. Goenka's [talk at] Donaldson. His words were inspirational. The experience of Dhamma is now my life. Just as Mr. Goenka said, "whatever purity you have attained, that should not only be maintained but must be increased, developed."

I miss all my Dhamma brothers. To be away from them and having to have to practice alone really is a test. Simply because of the new surrounding and the different negative mentality that is around me every day. I tell people of my blessing everyday. Sometimes it's hard to explain Vipassana to a bunch of guys who doesn't have a clue. Nevertheless I try. And they be interested because mainly of me. They (the ones who knew the old me) see the change in me. I hear this all the time; "Ed, you are not same." My response is one they don't understand. Well at least until I explain what I experienced.

Please know that I am keeping up my practice. If it wasn't for you staying on my case—I don't think I would've gotten the full effect of Vipassana.

Sometimes I look back and imagine how messed up my life once was, compared to the way I live now and smile. I finally have something to smile about. Now don't get me wrong—everything isn't all "peaches and cream" here. Like for instance; I got stressed dealing with my past involvement with the "gang" life & still having to have to explain my disassociation with them. I don't mind explaining though, because whether they like it or dump it, "I am happy & at peace with me now."

Edward

September 11 - October 22, 2002
The Addict's Mentality: Not Just Another Fix

"...be careful I wasn't just getting a rush" —James George

James George
September 11, 2002

Dear Dhamma Sister,

The day we broke Noble Silence [on day ten of the first ten- day course] we were talking and Bruce asked what inspired me to spend so much time in the 'Meditation Hall'. I told him I've always pushed myself to the limit in whatever I do. Then I mentioned that was why I had been such a hard-core addict, because I was compelled to do everything all out. He then told me to be careful that I wasn't using meditation as a substitute for drugs.

I must say, this shocked me at first. Then I began to think, well, he may be right, so I'd better pay attention. I decided to give myself a substantial period of time to assure myself that everything I experienced during Vipassana was real and not a passing fancy.

Now I can testify that my experiences were indeed real. I continue my practice daily. It has brought about tremendous changes in my life and my total outlook.

In fact, without this serenity I don't know what I would have done these last couple of days. Tuesday I was moved out of the Program. Not for anything I've done but because the Captain over treatment has absolutely no idea how treatment works.

I thank God for the four and a half years I've had in treatment. Without the concepts I've learned there, the tools I've
been given and all the wonderful insight I've gained working
with Ms. Johnson, coupled with the ability to obtain peace I
learned in Vipassana, I would probably be at wits end. However,
I can honestly say that I'm okay. Jenny, I don't even feel any
animosity toward Captain R.. I just remind myself that all is
impermanent.

Metta,

James

James George
September 24, 2002

Dear Jenny,

You are quite right, my daily life changed dramatically.
Being accustomed to the atmosphere of the Drug [Treatment]
Dorm, I was totally unprepared for the chaos I encountered in
the blocks. The noise level was unbelievable! It was practically
impossible to find a time quiet enough to meditate.

On Wednesday, the 18th, they moved me back to South Side
to H-dorm. This was done at around 9:00 p.m., right out of the
blue. Then on Monday they moved me from H-dorm to G-
dorm, again without any notice or reason. I don't even unpack
because they may move me again at a moment's notice.

Jenny, there are two things which get me through all of
this. # 1—From the Big Book Acceptance: "Acceptance is the
answer to all my problems today. When I am disturbed, it is
because I find some person, place, thing, or situation—some
fact of my life—unacceptable to me, and I can find no serenity
until I accept that person, place, thing, or situation as being
exactly the way it is supposed to be at this moment." #2—What
Goenkaji said during his discourse on the last day: "If you
practice Vipassana properly, a change must come for the better
in your life. You should check your progress on the path by

checking your conduct in daily situations, in your behavior and dealings with other people. Instead of harming others, have you started helping them? When unwanted situations occur, do you remain balanced?"

Every day is a new experience and I live it to its fullness, learning all I can from it. I stay focused on what I plan on doing when I get out. I am going to get into counselling. I want to do a book on my life experiences and I am going to speak anywhere anyone will listen about prison reform. This should keep me busy, don't you think?

Metta, James

James George
September 27, 2002

Dhamma Brother, [Bruce]

It has been 8 months since our Vipassana course and I have thought many times about writing. The reason I've waited is because of something you said the morning we broke noble silence.

The question came up what inspired me to work so hard, spending so much time in the 'Meditation Hall.' I didn't really know how to answer this, so I likened it to other things I've done, putting everything I had into it. I mentioned that like when I was a drug addict, I had to be a 'hard-core' addict.

At that point Bruce, you said something which caused me to do a great deal of reflection. You told me to be careful I wasn't just getting a rush, or something to that effect, and this caused me to do alot of soul-searching. I knew I had to discover the truth before I could ever be satisfied.

Thank you Bruce for making me search, for by doing so I discovered true panna, [wisdom] the understanding of reality as it is. My meditation has become deeper, my understanding more thorough and my acceptance far greater. The balance I have achieved is unbelievable. I am no longer overwhelmed by daily situations. I rather observe without reacting, acknowledge it for what it is and let it pass away. Equanimity!

Jenny said she told you about my current situation. Well, it has changed again, and again, and again...all is impermanent...On 9/10/02 I was moved from the Drug Dorm to 4-Block, a chaotic hell. On 9/18/02 I was moved from 4-Block back to South Side into H-Dorm. On 9/23/02 I was moved from H-Dorm next door to B-dorm. On 9/26/02 I was moved from B-dorm back to the Drug Dorm. And you want to know what's really funny about all this? I'm not the least bit perturbed about any of this. In fact I find it a great learning experience. So I once again thank you for raising a doubt about just how serious I was about my meditation. I've come so far in the last 8 months.

Several of us are praying you are allowed to bring Vipassana back.

Be happy, Be peaceful, Be liberated,
Metta, *James*

Bruce Stewart
October 22, 2002

Dear James:

I was very happy to receive your inspiring letter and learn of your progress in Dhamma. As you so correctly note, the benefits of Dhamma are tangible, deep, here and now. Equanimity is the only yardstick to measure our progress. Having a deep sense of gratitude and a desire to serve others are other Dhamma qualities that naturally percolate from within and further demonstrate that progress is certainly being made.

I was particularly interested in your response to the comments I made after your first course. I asked the question based on our past experience with those who struggle with substance abuse. Firstly, I wanted to assess what was driving you to work so diligently and, secondly, caution you about the dangers of approaching Vipassana with an "addict's mentality" and possibly using Vipassana as just another fix. It seems you understood my motive well and have carefully and sincerely examined your practice. The substantial results you have gained speak for themselves. Giving your practice the test of time was a wise move. There is no doubt in my mind that you are on the right track, and I encourage you to continue to sit as much as you can. As long as *upekkha* (equanimity) is constantly being cultivated along with the understanding of anicca (impermanence), you have nothing to be concerned about. Real equanimity and wisdom are only developed with this deepening understanding of anicca.

I'm sorry and disappointed to learn that your group sittings have been taken away from you all. I realize that this must be very difficult for you. The comradeship and support of your Dhamma brothers can be an additional bonus to your practice. However, I urge all of you not to generate negativity about this situation, but instead generate metta (loving-kindness) for those who implemented this unfortunate ruling. With the base of metta, a solution may present itself. While it would be ideal if you could all gather to sit together on a regular basis, remember that each one of you has the Dhamma deep inside. No one can take this away! Keep Dhamma strong by keeping your sittings strong and continue to develop the noble qualities of Dhamma: sila (morality), samadhi (concentration) and pañña (experiential wisdom).

Bruce

October 30, 2002
Support Letters to Pardon and Parole Board: Request Declined

"By maintaining this strict boundary, the students have no other motivation than to look deeply within themselves."—Bruce Stewart

Edward Johnson
October 30, 2002 *(continuation)*

[To Bruce]

Then there's the dealing with wanting my freedom back
that gets stressful also. I gave these people eleven and a half
years of my life. They have set my parole date off again and now
I don't know when I will go back up again. Regardless of what
is taking place in my life—I am finally at peace with myself.

My family is doing fine. My mother is really learning and
loving the technique of meditating. When I get home, her and
I are planning to take a course together. My son is twelve years
old now and I plan on getting him involved. Bruce, I miss my
family a great deal. I pray I am released soon. Then I will be
able to definitely spread the love and power of Dhamma.

Hey Bruce, before I forget, I have a favor to ask of you,
Jenny, Rick & Jonathan. Will you all write a letter of recom-
mendation for my release to Pardon & Parole Board for me?
You all have basically watched me change before your very
eyes. It's a question that needs attention as soon as possible.
I'm not asking you guys to lie for me. I am only asking you all
to let them know the effect of Dhamma and what you all see
in me. If you don't mind, you can send the letters to me on
my behalf and I will forward them to the Parole Board. I really
would be grateful!

Edward

Bruce Stewart
(undated)

Dear Edward:

I'm sorry to hear you have been shuffled around once
again—back with your Dhamma brothers at Donaldson for a

while and then moved to yet another camp. I hope that your next "camp" is a meditation center in the "free world."

I want to explain our policy regarding your request for support with your parole hearing. My reason for not wanting to get involved with your parole board hearing is based strictly upon the objectives and guidelines we have for our prison and jail courses. You know I would very much like to help, but we need to keep the bigger picture in mind in terms of our ongoing Vipassana programs.

Firstly, it is important for us to be completely neutral in our dealings with our inmate-students. In other words, we are there to facilitate the teaching of Dhamma, and we do not want to mix in any other incentive other than offering the pure and deep experience of the ten-day course. By maintaining this strict boundary, the students have no other motivation than to look deeply within themselves. In addition, the correctional facilities we deal with need to be assured that we are there for just one thing—the ten-day course and the ongoing support of the students' progress in their practice. We are not there to reform the institution or advocate for the inmates. Once again, we are there only to teach Dhamma! I trust you understand.

Edward, I wish you well in your continued growth in Dhamma and hope that one day soon we will see you here at Dhamma Dhara (Vipassana Meditation Center) sitting a course in the free world.

Bruce

March 2003
After One Year, How Does Dhamma Fare Inside?

"I think the Dhamma actually took root at Donaldson. It is a great honor to be one of the beneficiaries." —OB Oryang

John W. Johnson
March 9, 2003

Dear Bruce,

One year plus has passed since y'all Dhamma people came
to 'Bama. I can speak with absolute truth that this has been
an extraordinary year. Even with what in the past would have
been looked upon as a mundane day—it is one where Dhamma
serves to prelude the experience . . . .

For this insight—myself, and I am sure others—we are
eternally grateful.

Thank you all, also, for your last letter with instruction
on "truth as our island—truth as our refuge." I heard & hear
what you are saying. As always the insight of being skillful with
expression of Dhamma in a hostile environment takes practice,
as you stated in your last letter.

It is an area that I really need to cultivate. Non-harming
communication takes skill, especially in a hostile environment
where people are in such an emotional state of suffering.

The words of the Buddha on the four types of people we
learned about on the eighth day of the course have been a great
help to me.

Four types of people in the world: those who are running
from darkness towards darkness, those who are running from
brightness toward darkness, those who are running from
darkness towards brightness, and those who are running from
brightness towards brightness.

This along with the teaching of the law of [dependent
causation]'this arises depending on that,' I am able to see what
is going on. What would happen before was I would be caught
in the flow of reactions. It has also been helpful to remember
the teaching of "being careful not to justify your actions only
after the event." One must examine the mind before acting.

Prison is a good training ground for being aware of your
volitions. I see how easy ego creeps back in—taking "things"
personal—

My sitting practice is also in constant change. Somedays I am unable to keep my predetermined time to sit. When this happens I just accept it as "the way things are"—I do not try to control—just go with the flow with a serious determination to cultivate my Vipassana practice deeper. I further realize that Vipassana awareness is a part of my life at all times—while sitting and not sitting. Even in my sleep, dreams bring moments of awareness of sensations. I also am learning how to be more skillful at being stronger with the equanimity of the sensations.

John

Bruce Stewart
April 18, 2003

Dear John:

I'm very happy that you are so clearly moved by your experience in Dhamma and that, in spite of your challenging circumstances, you are keeping Dhamma strong. Maintaining your daily practice is the only way to do this! I encourage you to sit as much as you can. James George wrote me and said that he was going to do a "self-course" through the night. I never heard back from him on how it went, but the determination and tenacity he demonstrates is encouraging and commendable.

You speak of an "extraordinary year." Many would agree. Goenkaji's tour of North America was a unique happening and having him come to Donaldson at the conclusion of the May course certainly was a highlight for many of us. His visit touched thousands and we are seeing increased numbers apply for courses nationwide. In fact, most centers have large waitlists as we do here at the Vipassana Meditation Center, Dhamma Dhara, in Shelburne. There are new centers opening in Toronto and Chicago, with others in the works . . . so Dhamma is spreading. At Dhamma Dhara, we are about to start a new building project that should increase our capacity by more than forty.

Not only is Dhamma spreading in the "free world," but also in prisons and jails. Just recently Mexico and Spain had their first prison courses. Both paralleled our Donaldson experience with inmates working really hard and getting corresponding results. It seems that, worldwide, inmates are very responsive to the Buddha's profound yet simple teaching to alleviate suffering. Soon you will all receive the latest International Newsletter that features prison and jail courses around the world. Next week Jonathan and I will visit a women's prison in Vermont to look at a potential course site. A number of the administrative staff have attended the ten-day course, including the director of the facility. Hopefully we will get the go-ahead to hold a course in the not-too-distant future. It seems a prison in Baltimore is also at about the same stage, so we may be having courses there as well. However, we will have to wait and see as we have seen so many times in the past that there are often last-minute difficulties.

How are all the Dhamma Brothers doing? Has the administration allowed you to continue with your group sittings yet? I trust that you are all able to support each other to keep up your sitting either individually or in small groups in your dorms.

Bruce

John W. Johnson
March 13, 2003

The Way it is—Doing Time Doing Vipassana

The little booklet "Guidelines for Practicing Vipassana Meditation" given to me after the course has been intensely utilized. The information is very practical and useful to me a new student to become an old, serious student.

The Frequently Used Terms section has often opened the path for me—even when I may be going through some form of hindrance.

An area of the booklet that I have spent a considerable amount of time contemplating is the three kinds of wisdom:
- Wisdom gained by listening to others
- Intellectual, analytical understanding
- Wisdom based on direct personal experience

What I do is, I remember how my life experience is in a constant flux of change. This is wonderful now that I can experience change without fear and am learning the power of well-being by observing letting go of defilements.

I have explored how pañña (wisdom) is a part of my day. I examine the way pañña has been a part of my personal experience on the direct spectrum. It is part of my questioning of what I apprehend to be my own experiential reality. Otherwise, why practice Vipassana . . . one could just continue as a blind being. I guess once the blind see, there is no going back.

One of the ways I do battle with rebellious cravings and gain *bhavana-maya pañña* (experiential wisdom) with my everyday walking around practice, is to face my 'habitual attachments' for what they are, when they arise.

Example: Food—Pleasure craving for sweet snack knowing I have in my locker box the object of my craving and not reacting by eating it. I have been doing this with adhitthana (strong determination) for the past year. This practice has also been useful with other cravings that arise too.

Another example: *dosa* (aversion)

At the five gallon coffee pot in our dorm we have a mop pail to catch the water drop-off. People have a habit of throwing waste in the pail; you know paper from sugar packs, soup tops, etc. No one wants to dump this pail because it looks horrifying with yucky stuff. Everyone complains about it—but no one wants to take charge to keep it empty of dirty water & junk. I even would wonder why no one would empty it before it fills the brim.

I finally thought . . . what am I doing?? Where is this aversion taking me? Now each day I empty it. I watch other aversions that arise in my day and do what I [need to, to address each] mental defilement. This form of walking around practice has helped me experience liberation in many other situations that arise in my dorm.

Prisoners are greatly accustomed to certain patterns of behavior. This is where *moha* (ignorance) comes into play. Unconsciously, we prefer the familiarity of chaos and the suffering in our lives. Even after cutting through the intense, habitual and occupying attachments we saw at a ten-day course, peace still appears to be a part of uncertainty.

For me it has not been easy. What continues is I am a very curious person by nature. By being able to gain from a direct personal experience a deepening awareness of the Dhamma as truth to the way things are at this moment—keeps me willing to continue this Vipassana practice. I look at how this training is awakening me to being human.

After years of being a slave to likes & dislikes, it is very interesting flowing with Dhamma—even while doing life without parole.

John

Rick Smith
April 15, 2003

Dear Jenny,

Since our last communication I had an interesting trip to lock-up. What was really neat was the obvious "real" reason for it. Guess how long I stayed? 11 days & 10 nights. A Vipassana. God really blessed me. Again, I was served each day & allowed to travel inward & just be with myself. I honestly got more out of that retreat than the one I did in May. I was due another & life looked out for me. Very little distractions. I had tremendous insights into resentments I had been storing up & my lack of focus/direction. There has been a shift for me. Most welcome.

My Transactional Analysis classes & Men's Work classes are going better than ever. I am so fortunate to live the life I lead. It's so meaningful to me.

As I'm sure James George has probably conveyed to you, the Alabama Prison System is definitely going thru some changes called "over-crowding." We are certainly hanging in there, but it is going to be challenging this summer when the heat gets here.

I am still sitting. I lead the morning meditation each morning into the Vipassana technique & give them a lot of information about Vipassana as well as I can. Even for the few minutes they use it they seem to benefit from it & enjoy it. [*This was under the auspices and guise of another class Rick was leading.*]

'Namaste'
Rick

Edward Johnson
April 16th, 2003

Dear Jenny,

I am steadily holding on with my head held high—in spite of all the negative distraction that surrounds me. It is close to summer again & the weather is beautiful. I would give anything just to be able to be on the other side of the fence, go to the park, stretch my blanket out and just meditate . . . Taking in the fresh air & listening to the sounds of birds chirping. Now that is a peaceful thought. I try to keep my mind on positive scenarios, things like that, in order to stay focused in this jungle. Thanks to Vipassana, I've learned how to stay on the straight and narrow.

Jenny—you, Bruce, Rick & Jonathan—have became a driving force of inspiration in my life. I talk about you all the time. Just as I do about Dr. Marshall. She is the one who helped bring my life & mental strength up to par. That is why I will always & forever cherish our relationship. A Dhamma relationship is an unbreakable bond.

Edward

Edward Johnson
May 8, 2003

Dear Jenny,

All of you: Bruce, Jonathan, Rick, Robin & you, have showed me—or better yet—have brought me into a beautiful world from which I thought I was lost. A world of Peace & Comfort. I never knew that the Power Dhamma could ever be so strong. It's a world of pure, genuine love. It's a world and way of life that I will never & could never turn away from. Dhamma is my life. Anger had consumed me for so many years. It was destroying me slowly. If I hadn't taken that step—with your help—I would still be lost in a world where there was/is no peace. That day in January 2002 was the day "Edward" (me) had showed people the Real me.

Sincerely,
Edward

John W. Johnson
May 18, 2003

The Way it is—Doing Time Doing Vipassana.

It was one year ago, around the end of May. I was walking around inside the dorm, still vibrating with subtle sensation. After all, I had only been back for around one week from the second ten day course at Donaldson.

In the continuous flux of noise that a prisoner who lives with 129 other convicts hears each day, I heard someone say, "Hey, there is a little rabbit outside the dorm. Let's go outside and look at it."

Fear swept into my mind. I was frightened for that little rabbit. I remember a few years ago that someone caught and tried to make one a pet. It died!! I remember that rabbit, and the fear it had in its eyes. Its heart beating so hard you could see his whole body moving. I felt so sorry for that rabbit and its panic in the hands of its captors. I surely did not want to see it now—not after the image of the last rabbit in my mind.

Someone said, "John!! Don't you want to see the rabbit?" I said, "Thanks, but no thanks." I did not tell them I was frightened. It was just stuff going on with me—inner voices of doubt & fear.

A few days later, one morning after our 5:00 a.m. group sitting—I was walking around the yard doing my job assignment, picking up litter. I love this job. I wear shower sandals and even sometimes walk around in the grass in my bare feet. It is always after the morning meditation.

It is a time when I become mindful of nature, of Dhamma.

Off at a distance in some grass that has not been cut for around two weeks, I saw a brown object . . . I was wondering what it could be. When it comes to litter in a prison yard you never know what you may find. So I walked in that direction. As I got closer I saw what looked to be a mixed brown color, kind of sandy, I guess.

When I got around fifteen feet away from the object I saw its ears—it was the rabbit. It was very still, I guess it thought it was hidden in the grass. I stood in amazement. I could not believe I was looking at a rabbit inside the prison compound.

People who were walking around the exercise path would walk past it not even noticing it. I asked one person, "Hey, look over there—it's a little cottontail rabbit." They said, "Yeah, we know, we have seen it before." I stood in awe. To me this was a remarkable event. Inside this prison compound known as the "House of Pain" sat a little cottontail rabbit. I wondered how it got into this yard. I wondered if it would be able to get through the fence again. We have an electric fence to keep prisoners from escaping—how could a little rabbit be protected from being killed by the fence?

The next day I went back to perform the duties of my prison job, that I never thought to be mundane, that is for sure, after all it was a job where I could walk bare foot to do my prison job. The Vipassana practice has opened up my mind to each moment of the day. The walking in nature, observing nature inside of me and outside of me has taken on much more depth. But now that I had seen this rabbit I wondered if I would see it again.

Well yes I did, in fact for around two weeks. I saw this rabbit grow from around five inches to about ten inches. I saw it sit inside a coil of razor wire. I thought that this young rabbit was a "silly rabbit." It must have thought that coil of wire was brushes and it camouflaged him. One day I saw someone throw a stone at him. He hopped just enough to move away a little. He did not seem to put much concern into an insensitive human being trying to scare him away.

I wondered in my mind what would be the fate of this rabbit. Would it grow too big to make his way through the fence? He looked fat to me. Then one day I saw him stretch his body out long and go through the fence with ease. I was amazed and very happy to see the rabbit was not a prisoner from ignorance of youth and would not be trapped inside like we were—young people who grow old inside the prison fence. We were young once and made bad choices, only to become captive. Captive from desire.

I remember when I no longer saw the rabbit again. I knew in my heart that it was time for him to go. I thought about the fear that arose in me, in my confusion about nature I doubted that the rabbit would be o.k. In my past experience of a rabbit I thought it would meet the fate of being taken as a pet to the amusement of a convict wanting to grasp at holding it from being free—only to die in fear. I did not want this to happen again.

In retrospect, I see it was my own fear from a past conditioning. My internal dialogue—fear and anxiety—was adversely controlling my experience. Even after "thinking" I have two ten-day [Vipassana] courses now, and I am in a state of awareness to the "way things are." In truth, I know nothing! Dhamma is continuously presenting awareness in a process. It is not a "state" to be in, with a "knowing." Knowing only becomes "solid"—it was shown that my awareness had dissipated when I had fear for that rabbit—based upon a past experience.

I had become a "silly rabbit," or "monkey minded," by allowing fear to grip a hold with a subtle fluctuation from awareness of the way things are.

So from the Dhamma lesson with the guru rabbit, I see how easy it is to allow ego to blind awareness and remove insight from the process of just realizing the experience without attachment to the "process."

Got to go it is getting late.

John

Edward Johnson
May 20, 2003

Dear Jenny,

Well I guess by now you have heard of the cancellation concerning my parole hearing. It hit me pretty hard. So I had to sit with it for about 10 days in straight meditating by myself. I am fine now. I knew it would be best that I did that because I never wanna lose focus. Plus why not use the technique which helped me to get back to normalcy. Although it wasn't the same without the "chants," you, and all my Dhamma brothers. I just visioned the chants & heard 'em in my head.

This letter will not be complete if I don't comment on the article I received off the internet about the progress of Vipassana at Donaldson. I was very elated to read it & see me, Ice and the brothers meditating.

I am still having to come to grips with the way they have treated me...by locking me up in Segregation for nothing. I mean Jenny...to do all the Right things in here and having

made the complete "360-degree turnaround" from a problem
to a model prisoner. Preparing myself for what lies ahead in
society. One thing I do know is they can't never take away what
I've found. And that, my dear, is peace, love & some beautiful
friends.

Your Dhamma Brother,
Edward

June 24, 2003
Wishes to a Dhamma Friend on a Course

*"Know you're in our thoughts, and we send you hope and metta to
get through."*—Michael Carpenter

John Johnson
June 24, 2003

Dear Jenny,

Jenny, I have been sending "metta" to you and ya'll at
Shelburne center. Also, have been daily reading a "Discourse
Summary" for each day that you have been there. You are a
very fortunate person to be able to take a second course. It is
so inspiring to me, and my practice…to see you move through
the "free-world" with such an encyclopedic ability for helping
others—but yet, you realize the importance to sit for ten days
doing Vipassana!!

Just being human is to be limited, conditioned and unique.
Each of us is shaped with vicissitudinous experiences, albeit
from cultural, historical and interpersonal forces. Vipassana
cuts through the concatenation that is the same in all of
us—"we suffer from becoming", or "being human." It is just
that simple, but such a complex "thing" without a practice and
path.

So as I do time—doing Vipassana—people like you inspire
me at the core of insight that springs fourth with a Dhamma in

my consciousness. Thank you for the awakening of a kindred
relationship with happiness.

Bhavatu sabba mangalam
(may there be every happiness)
metta, *John*

Michael Carpenter
June 24, 2003

Jenny,

    John told me you are going through your second Vipassana.
I guess most people would wish you a wonderful experience.
Having gone through it though, I know there's not much
wonderful about it. It's hard, painful, and emotionally devastating. But after we see the results, we can realize how wonderful
it was to be able to experience ourselves at the rawist. I remember my first day of actual Vipassana meditation. I started crying
about 25 minutes in to it and had to stop and sit there crying
until the sitting was over. As soon as it was, I jumped up and
ran to my bed, pulling a blanket over me crying. A few seconds
later, Bruce tapped me. I looked at him and he asked "Had a
hard one?" I replied, "Yes" with a smile. Then he smiled and
said "Good!" and walked away. It made me so angry. I felt how
could someone show so little compassion. I cried for 3 days.
But afterward I realized what Bruce meant and the next time I
saw him I had to thank him.

    So, I hope you have very hard sittings and hope you're able
to get so much more out of it. I learned so much about my self
in the one Vipassana I'm rather envious of you going into your
second. I hope I have that chance soon.

    Know you're in our thoughts, and we send you hope and
metta to get through.

Love,
Michael Carpenter

Edward Johnson
June 24, 2003

Greetings Jenny,

You are in the sixth day of your meditation [course]. After today, you will have four more days left to work.

On this day you should have developed awareness and equanimity towards sensations—the four elements and their relations to sensations. The four causes of the arising of matter—the five hindrances: craving, aversion, mental-and-physical sluggishness, agitation, doubt . . .

Jenny in four more days you can eradicate some of the mental defilements, and grasp the technique in order to make use of it throughout your life. I really wish I was there to see your refreshness as you walk out. It truly would be a wonderful sight to see. I can't wait to hear from you about your experience.

I also received a pamphlet about the new construction at the Vipassana center in Shelburne. Will you please tell me how I can donate my own money? This is something I truly want to do. It may not be much because of the situation I'm in. But I'm sure every dollar counts. I wanna see that the construction happens. Because it'll help thousands of people. . .Just as it did me.

Well, momma is doing fine. I believe she misses you. She said she is praying that you make it through your course.

Much metta,
Edward

John Johnson
July 13, 2003

Hello Jenny,

I had already been showered with a few "tidbits" about your course—via some Dhamma brothers around drug [treatment] dorm & Ms. Johnson. The prison "grapevine" is still alive.

So you liked the rabbit story. It is interesting to share this with you too. At first I felt a little shy with talking about the rabbit guru. I guess it is part of the fear I face, you know, "what will people think about me getting insights watching a rabbit?" As you can tell, though, that rabbit made a lasting impression on my consciousness one year after our encounter. It is also interesting that I wrote you that letter after "lights-out" time. I was having to strain my eyes to write you that letter.

I will be glad to share more insights with you about that encounter with my consciousness while observing the rabbit. This week I will put together reflections, o.k.?

For now I would like to share some insights your card brought me. Suffering, (dukkha) depth! You made note about suffering and the normal type: bodily pain, discomfort born from the adjustment to sitting for long time back to back and the heat during the summer months.

What really gives the power of doing Vipassana in prison a perfect setting. It is a place where so many people experience appearance of all the aggregates—sorrow, lamentation, distress, despair—the Noble Truth is opened up so deeply with people who suffer from <u>association</u> with the <u>unbeloved</u>, and with separation from the loved. You were very correct, prisons are maybe different from other types of courses—although, we might be surprised if we could read the minds of other people who take the courses. We all truly do suffer greatly.

I am very happy to have a practice that has opened up my heart to Dhamma. A very great opportunity came to Donaldson facility. A place where the appearance of the aggregates is no longer seen as permanent—Dhamma teaches it is penetrable by letting go of attachments.

Experience has shown us here that this is not just a "self-help theory" read in a book. This is the sweet fruit of the actual practice.

Metta,
John

October 2003
Vipassana and Christianity and Islam

"... take advantage of this wonderful, scientific, nonsectarian technique. Nobody asked you to convert yourself from one organized religion to another organized religion. The conversion is, rather, the conversion of the mind from bondage to liberation, from ignorance to enlightenment, from cruelty to compassion, from misery to happiness. This is required by one and all."—S.N. Goenka

"I saw through Vipassana that I was not giving near as much attention and awareness to my salat [five daily Islamic prayers] that I could and should, and that I would be getting much more from it if I did. I compared the attention and awareness I was able to develop through Vipassana and I said, 'Wow, I haven't been giving this much attention to my salat, you know, and here I almost didn't participate in Vipassana because I didn't want to forego my five salats a day.'" —Omar Rahman

"I wanted rehabilitation over a whole lot of defects in my life. My attitude for one, my sense of respect for others was low—even though I sincerely believed in God, I still didn't have what I needed to live peacefully regardless of conditions (prison)."—Willie Carroll

Edward Johnson
October 7, 2003

Dear Jenny,

It has been a while since I have actually picked up my pen & penned you a nice letter. There have been days where I have been wanting to, but my frame of mind wouldn't allow me to write unless it was all pleasantry.

Like right now Jenny, I basically just need some advice. The kind of advice to help me on my quest for Liberation. The great S.N. Goenkaji spoke of liberation. That liberation can be gained only by practice, never by mere discussion. Jenny, that is what I am battling with right now...Practice & Discussion!!!

See, I not too long ago just come out of a week long sitting with myself. It felt different. Don't get me wrong, it felt good to practice Vipassana. It's the not being able to share the experience with someone who'd understand. These people don't know and I be trying to enlighten them—but as soon as I mention Buddha & Pali (the original language of Buddha)—they get spooked...as if I am trying to change their minds or belief toward their religions. However, some or rather a great deal of these people have noticed the tremendous change I have made in my life. What they don't/didn't know was about the technique which helped me to find my way. It's a struggle, I must say. But it's a struggle that is worth every bit of energy I have in my soul. Sometimes I wished they'd understand...without the misunderstanding about Dhamma. I know I am going to continue to follow Dhamma. It is what changed my life. And I will never be afraid to share my experience with anybody.

Jenny, I miss my Dhamma family at Donaldson. I also miss you, Jenny, and Rick, Jonathan & Bruce. You guys really does not know how much Love & Peace you have brought to my life. In the process of the love & Peace that has developed within me, there are stumbling blocks that are set before me by an administration who chooses not to accept the man that I am or rather have become thru the help of Vipassana. Again, like I said previously, it's a struggle—one that is worth every energy I have in my soul.

Well, enough about me right now. I am ready to travel the world to show everybody the remarkable work of Vipassana.

Stay Genuine & Focused,

Edward

Omar Rahman
October 7, 2003

Dear Jenny

May this be a good day for you. Because of you, I experience more good days than I have known during the whole of my incarceration. It was a joy to hear from you. Writing back has been like swimming through molasses. I've been full with clutter. Not only this environment but also that which this environment engenders inside. Between the time that you wrote me and now I got better at emptying my bowl. I read Sue Bender's book "Everyday is Sacred" in the meantime and I was able to bring more clarity to my experience. I finished yesterday and I feel fresh, Jenny. It was an enjoyable and insightful read. I read it with a bowl of oatmeal or a cup of coffee, and a pillow, while sitting in a corner of the field each morning.

Jenny, you, Robin [Casarjian], Bruce and Jonathan have enhanced my life immensely. The value you have given to my experience of life is greater than that of all the Monets, Manets and Van Goghs of the world.

I am more caring. I am kinder. I am more gentle with myself and others. I forgive much easier now. I am happier Jenny. I have perceptional skills I heretofore didn't have, especially of what was happening within me. I have skillful means to manage my experience more effectively.

The experience of the ten-day course and all that it has opened my life to has broadened and deepened the whole of my life experience.

You asked me how has it enriched my Islam faith. Well I'll tell you over the past couple of years I've read more books by Buddhist monks, scholars and authors than I have of Islamic scholars & authors. The information I've received from Buddhist writers has enabled me to touch and feel my personal experience in a way that has not been afforded to me from any other source.

Experiencing openness and learning to open myself more has allowed me to access more of the space of my existence.

When an adverse occurrence arises around me I'm less reactive because I have space to see and act with skill. I'm less caught up in anger when it flares or any other negative feelings. I'm less hooked if you will. I can let go. I have more space within me to be otherwise. I can let go and be kind, or let go and be forgiving. I can let go because I have the power to do so.

What you all placed in my bowl was what I needed at that time, more so than anything else.

You, Robin, Bruce & Jonathan, through your vision, your teachings, your support, your caring and your sincere concern have altered my life forever. Reality will never be the same.

I hope you don't tire of my long-winded writings because I'm not through talking to you. I have enjoyed our talk and I'm honored that you take the time to "hear me out."

Metta,
Omar

Interview with Omar Rahman

Jenny: **Has Vipassana informed your Islam practice in any way?**

Informed immensely, immensely. I understand more of what I'm doing. In my salat, which is the particular prayer that you do in Islam, you get away from everything, and at this particular time you let everything else go. You detach yourself from everything and you focus. I saw through Vipassana that I was not giving near as much attention and awareness to my salat that I could and should, and that I would be getting much more from it if I did. I compared the attention and awareness I was able to develop through Vipassana and I said, "Wow, I haven't been giving this much attention to my salat, you know, and here I almost didn't participate in Vipassana because I didn't want to forego my five salats a day. [But] in going through Vipassana I realize that I was not giving [or] utilizing salat as much as I should to get the benefit from it that I should. Vipassana brought this to my mind.

Did you struggle with not doing your five salats a day during the ten days?

No, not after I committed myself, because my focus was upon truth and it was an honest focus; it was for spiritual growth and development. It was sincere on my part and I was really comfortable with that. Muslim brothers were asking me about it and I said, well, that is something that I resolved within myself. And I would ask any other Muslim brother to resolve that issue within himself. In regards to salat, that was the advice I gave. I would give them my experience. I would tell them Vipassana was very, very beneficial and it would not take anything from you; it would give to you, it would enhance everything. Friday is a particular religious day, and on that day I give an hour talk and we participate in community salat. I haven't told them, but much of the understanding of the Qur'an that I've been giving to them has come from the understanding I have gotten from Vipassana. I've been able to go into the Qur'an and understand on a wider level.

Can you give an example, Omar?

Sometimes you like something that gives you harm and you dislike the thing that gives you benefit. There is a particular phrase in the Qur'an in that we should check our likes and dislikes. This means, to me, craving and aversion. This was identically the same thing that was being said in the Qur'an: that you should guide your heart because you may like something that brings you harm and you may dislike something that brings you good. There's a phrase which says, "Check your appetites with your intelligence." You don't just give a seed to gratify your appetites without any restraint. Craving, craving—you check that with intelligence. You ask yourself, "Would this be good for me in this capacity or would it be harmful? Would this be good for someone else or would it be of harm?"

In the Qur'an there's a word *mizan,* and it means balance. Balance is a sign that is sent down to you from up high—mizan—you must have balance in all things. And so when I get to equanimity—balance—this is the first thing comes to my mind. I've been teaching the need for one to have balance within one's life. I've gone to the point of bringing out how important it is you have balance [in] how you react to things, whether it is in your like or your dislike or your wants, or the things that you don't want. If one has been through Vipassana they would say, "Oh that sounds like Vipassana," but it's also Qur'an, it is also Islam. I found a correlation and I felt the reality of a dhamma, a certain truth here. I saw that truth and I tried to relate that. I try to tell them that there's more than ritual; there's an experience that you must become a part of. I told them I take the salats over and over again but if you are just saying words and bowing—you are just going through positions—you're missing it. I think Vipassana has given me something that would help them get beyond just the ritual of their practices.

Omar Rahman
(undated)

Dear Jonathan,

There was a period in my life [when] I learned more about myself from Buddhist writers than I did from Islamic writers, specifically in regards to the emotional interior. I wanted a map of that place. Although Islamic thought places a major emphasis on human compassion, human kindness and love, this emphasis among the writers has appeared more doctrinal and intellectual. However, Buddhist writings on the same subject matter were more experiential in tone and substance in that, instead of just defining what compassion, kindness or forgiveness is, those writings describe what they feel like.

When talking about the emotional well being of a person, from Islamic writers I get a table of contents and from the Buddhist writers I learn what those contents feel like.

Although Islam has given me a positive in terms of how I perceive reality and how I perceive myself, yet there were emotional issues that were not being resolved that I wanted information about.

I wanted to know where all my anger was coming from. Why was I so irritated? Why were there long periods of emotional emptiness in my life? Why am I so hung up on this or crave that, obsessed with this or stuck on that? I wanted information that would show me where I was on the interior landscape, how I got there and how to navigate that landscape.

Islam does light a path through the interior landscape of the human experience; however, I have not encountered Islamic writers who illuminate the details of that landscape as [have] Buddhist writers. One other quality of Buddhist writers that has been a benefit to me is the inclusion of feeling as a faculty of how one can know and understand one's experience. This was important to me because knowing through rational thought alone had not taken me the final mile to where my issues were. But learning how to feel where I was, then learning how to identify what I was feeling and why I was feeling as I did paved the way for me being able to manage my life in a much more skillful way.

Heretofore I was without these bearings, markers, directions and insights. Most of my emotional sufferings have diminished or I know more about why I was suffering because of what I have learned through Buddhist teachings and practices.

Because of Vipassana I now see dimensions of Islam in ways I hadn't before. One example is metta. I was blown away by the "practice of feeling others, of caring about the suffering of others, and caring about the happiness of others." The idea of being able to enlarge this capacity within myself through practice had eluded me. What was so startling about it to me was that I'd been reading year in year out the same thing in my Qur'anic studies and studies on the teachings and practices of Prophet Muhammad. Case in point, there is a verse in the Qur'an that describes a sincere Muslim. It includes all the required religious practices, however these practices are mentioned after it is stated how important it is to care about the orphan, the indigent or the homeless people who are suffering. Throughout the Qur'an caring about those who are suffering is tied to identity. So while being taught metta I said to myself, "Whoa, your book has been telling you this for years, Omar, but you are just now getting it." Then there is the statement by Prophet Muhammad that a good Muslim desires for others what he desires for himself which echoed in my mind when I was sharing my love, my peace and my happiness with all beings. There was another time when a man asked Prophet Muhammad who among them was the best Muslim. He answered, "The best of you are those who are most kind to their wives." Not most knowledgeable mind you, nor most perfect in prayers or other religious acts, but who expressed the most kindness. What he was saying didn't fully touch me until Vipassana increased my awareness of the value of loving kindness. One night during the Vipassana course, before I fell asleep, I said to myself, "Omar, Buddha has made you a better Muslim."

During the Vipassana course, I was fortunate to be able to develop strong determination in my sitting meditation. As a consequence, I was able to develop strong determination in my observance of my prayers. I must admit that at the close of the Vipassana course, my observance in my meditation was keener than what my observance had been in my prayers. Realizing this, I began to bring that same quality of mindfulness and determination to my prayers.

As an Imam and having taken the Vipassana course, I began to emphasize the importance of being observant and attentive. For instance, the Qur'an constantly mentions the importance of being mindful and observant of what is in the heart. Prior to the Vipassana course, these were words of wisdom. After Vipassana these words became a practice. Also I constantly remind those I talk to how valuable and important it is to be able to direct our attention to what others are feeling and experiencing. I try to instill a sense of value on caring about others. Now, I am a much more tolerant, patient, and forgiving person in my relationships. I have shared what I have experienced in Vipassana with other Muslims. I have related how meaningful the experience is to me and how grateful I am for being able to have taken the course. I try to give other Muslims a "feel" of my experience and what I have learned so that they may have a reference to base their decision of whether they would like to take the course.

My devotion to Islam grew out of how Islam helped me to become conscious of how valuable I am as a person. I come out of a family and community that were beset with the mental and emotional conditionings and patterns of behavior that accompany low personal esteem and low personal worth. Vipassana directed my attention to the sense of basic goodness of all human beings and this resonated with the sense of value [that] Islam enlightened.

I believe there is a psycho-emotional state underlying the African-American experience that manifests a "something is wrong with me" condition. The Dhamma can be a source of healing for this condition. Dhamma teachers who are aware of this existing condition can be very effective by emphasizing those aspects of Dhamma that relate to personal worth.

Metta, *Omar*

Interview with Larry Singletary

Jenny: Did you do some other programs after you got out of the drug unit?

Yeah, I took Houses of Healing. I moved to the honor community. They have a structured environment in there. I'm taking Stress Management and Anger Management now. Of course I did Vipassana, but I think I learned more in Vipassana about myself than anything.

Can you talk about it and just tell me how it happened that you learned so much about yourself?

By going through it, listening to the tapes with Goenka and learning about what you're made of and the sensation thing. You learn a lot about little things that goes on everyday with your body that you really don't pay attention to. But they're all there and once you become aware of 'em, then it's just after a while it becomes normal too—all the sensations—but you know the reason for 'em. I believe that's a good thing too. Of course, I like doing my meditation by myself. I've kinda always been like that, you know. At one time I liked to hang out in crowds but, as I got older, it seemed like I'd rather be by myself alone a lot. And I'm more comfortable meditating by myself.

How do you feel now?

When somebody says something to me now, I think before I react. I put my mind into the mode of thinking when somebody comes up and starts talking to me, whatever it's about. I've had people come up, be angry about something and I can see that they're angry, so I automatically go into just thinking about, "I wonder why he's so mad, you know?" Where before, he would come up and present an anger image to me, I would automatically try to double that image back on him. But that's the way we deal with situations in here. Now it's just like one guy told me the other night, he said, "Man," he said, "you just sat like I wasn't even talking to you. It just went right by you." I said, "Yeah, right through me, more or less, you know." I said, "I don't want you to get mad."

But you were feeling less peaceful about it before Vipassana?

Yeah. Stayed agitated a lot, you know, angry, and that didn't help, that didn't help any. It makes it worse really. By going through Vipassana it actually helped because now I don't really get stressed out about it or be angry or nothing. A lot of times after I went through the Vipassana I observed people in different ways than before I took it, you know. And sometimes I really feel sorry for some people, where before I wouldn't feel sorry. You know, I'd say, "Well, he brought that on himself," or something. Now instead of that it's "Well, you know, maybe he don't know any better," or something like that. I hope they continue that here. I mean, if everytime they have it, if they help two or three people, that's a great help here. That's two or three more people they gonna help. But I'll be able to help more people now.

It was supposed to be a refuge from the rest of the prison.

Well, it was. But I know three or four of the guys were from different gangs. I said, when I first saw them come in there together, I know they wasn't going to work it out. I know they weren't going to make it.

You're saying that there were actually two men from opposing gangs?

Uh huh! And they were friendly—by the end of Vipassana, they were friendly. Before that, out here in the population, they weren't friendly.

You think more and more people would take it?

Yeah, I believe they would. There's been a lot of people questioning us about it, asking about how they can maybe take it, get on a list and take it. You know there's a lot of interest in it.

Why were people so interested in it? What do you think they saw?

Well, one thing is, we all came out and they saw something in us. Or saw something that [used to be] in us that wasn't there anymore or whatever. Then that just got their interest up, and a lot of people that's in prison are looking for something.

What do you think they are looking for?

They're just. . . you're trying to find something about. . . one thing is, why you're here, who you are, where you're going, why did you come here—things like that.

Those are pretty big questions aren't they?

Yeah. You always. . . you got this crowd out there, somebody talking about God this, or Mohammed this. You know that's the two major things here—God and Mohammed—and you hear that so long. And you see this guy over here talking the Bible every day, talking about God, but then that night or the next day you see him doing something somebody else is doing, and you wonder about, "Well, what's that all about?" So, you have a lot of people that don't fall off into that—but they're searching for something you know, I guess a thread of reality or something to latch on to. And ten days of Vipassana is a thread of reality. You have the reality and realize who you are and what you are, what you can be, you know, things like that.

Can you say something about that, Larry? What are some of your realizations about those big questions: "Who am I? Where am I going? Why am I here?"

I feel like I am a part of nature and that I'm going wherever my road is destined to take me, and I know where I'm going. I'm going back as one with nature when I leave here and I never realized that before. I guess it would be all right, you know, if some of those guys, you know, believing in God... well, that's cool. But I don't believe that if there's a God, that I'm going with God. I believe that I'm going back where I came from, and I know that I came from the earth, nature. 'Cuz it tells you in the Bible that you came from the earth, and the earth is nature, it's a part of nature. So you know it's... I feel like I got a good idea who I am.

November 2003 to November 2004
Underground: Group Sittings by Any Other Name

"Things will change for the better one day. Until then, I'll continue doing what I can to better myself and offer the best I can to my brothers, and to life itself." —Willie Carroll

John Johnson
November 2, 2003

Dear Jenny,

The card with the photo of what I 'assume' is the Concord River really touched me. It looks so serene. I took a journey of chimerical thoughts to each part of the photo—even to wondering about the people who took the 'shot' and the handrail of a boat in the lower left hand corner. It is very understandable that there was a river that inspired Emerson.

Which brings to mind—this week I received some information from the Sturge Weber Foundation—they are a foundation that is doing research to help with hope for families of a child with Sturge-Weber syndrome or port wine stain birthmarks to have a brighter future. I tell you, Jenny, it was quite an experience to see photos of people with birthmarks just like mine. Never had this happened for me out of my fifty-three years of life.

Now to answer your question on group sittings. No one has said we can do Vipassana group sittings. I keep hopeful though. At this time we only have two to four people who are willing to come to our Wednesday "New Solutions" group. This is the time slot allotted for a meditation group. We have a one hour and fifteen minute weekly slot to listen to tapes on meditation practices and to actually meditate as a group. I look at it as a start toward someday being allowed to have "Vipassana Group Sittings." Of course I still do Vipassana meditation without tapes.

I have this year been in contact with some of the people of the Vipassana Community of Abhayagiri Sangha. They have offered me a very good selection of free distribution books. I am very thankful for having been blessed with locating some "dana" gifts of generosity. These books have helped me greatly in learning about people around the world who practice Vipassana.

So, Jenny, life is much more auspicious here at Donaldson since the teachings of Vipassana came. Even though we do not any longer have group Vipassana meditation—Vipassana is still here, and an active part of our lives.

Got to go now. Y'all take care.

Metta, *John*

Benjamin Oryang
December 8, 2003

My Dear Friend,

I am burning up. It is 24 degrees outside, but around 85 in my cell. This is the true meaning of going from one extreme to the other. Just two weeks ago we were complaining about the lack of heating in the cell-blocks. Now that the heat is here in full swing, we are complaining about the lack of cold in the cell-blocks. If by some stroke of genius the temperature is regulated at about 70 degrees, we will find something else to complain about (like the texture of the bread in the dining hall or the sound of the intercom announcing for church services and interrupting our sleep).

When I say "we" I mean the residents of the cell-blocks as a whole, but there are some prisoners who can be excluded from that majority. Many of our Dhamma brothers, whether or not they are active with the group sittings, fall in the category of what in here is called the "laid-back" kind. This is encouraging in light of the fact that many of us were rowdier than the average prisoner at Donaldson before our ten-day sittings. I think the Dhamma actually took root at Donaldson. It is a great honor to be one of the beneficiaries.

We had a sitting last Wednesday in the group room. Though short, we were able to use the CD with the opening and closing by Goenkaji. There were only eight people present but the chanting filled in for all the rest.

The letters and books from Pariyatti arrived early last week. I have here with me one of the books, "The Moon Appears When the Water Is Still" by Ian McCrorie, and intend to start reading it tonight. As you had hoped, the correspondence has enlivened a sense of connection to Rick, Bruce and Jonathan, and to the practice. We are all very fortunate to have them—and you, Jenny. Though the Dhamma cannot be credited to any single being, it is only through your efforts that it came to Donaldson. Without overlooking the contributions from several other people, I recognize your part here; you are appreciated very much. And you are in my heart.

OB

Benjamin Oryang
January 10, 2004

Dear Jenny,

HAPPY NEW YEAR!! "The Moon Appears When The Water Is Still" is a wonderful book. I plan to read it again in the future, after the other Dhamma brothers have had a chance to read it too. Right now I am half way through one of the other books—"Realizing Change: "Vipassana Meditation in Action" by Ian Hetherington. The book is well written. I would recommend it equally for both Vipassana meditators and people who have never heard of the technique before.

In the past six months, I have seen more people get out of prison at Donaldson than in the preceding 129 months of my stay here. This comes as no surprise as the state of Alabama is in some deep difficulties: the prisons are overflowing, yet the system is financially incapable of carrying the load. I wish that I could somehow slip through the cracks and get out of here too, but with all likelihood there will be numerous objections from the Alabama Victims Rights Association—which has an office at the Alabama State House and a member (or two) on the Alabama Board of Pardons and Parole. I have always wondered how I could get in touch with the families and victims of the crimes I was convicted of committing, without inciting any fear, pain, anger or hatred in them, to tell them that I am not a murderer and to beg them not to protest my release in the event that I have a parole hearing. After all the suffering they have endured and after all the fingers of blame which have been pointed in my direction, including many of my own mistakes, it is hard to think that they could ever believe that I have never killed or even attempted to kill anyone in my life. That is why it feels as though contacting them will only cause them more misery, and spark renewed energy to protest any mention of my release. Please tell me what you think.

Please write back soon. And keep warm. I understand that it is pretty cold up there. The same is true here for this climate, but the heaters are working just well for my liking: it is cool and I have on a sweater. You are in my heart.

OB

Edward Johnson
May 9, 2004

Dear Jenny,

I am feeling kind of down at the moment, but I had to come out of seclusion & reach out to touch my Dhamma sister. Today is Mothers Day. I pray yours was a laid back one. Then again to me, everyday is Mothers Day...Nevertheless I am still going to follow the script & wish you a Happy Mothers Day with much metta.

Jenny I would like to Thank You from the bottom of my heart for the Gift. Although I needed really bad, for cosmetics

& Food, there was no way I could bring myself to ask you for it. You just don't know how much it meant to me.

The system is once again trying to make me go backwards. I was placed in Segregation because I said something to my Cell partner about his bad Hygiene Habits...At least that's what they said. The warden (Garrett) came over to Seg. & released me himself. I was surprised!!! He said it himself that disciplinary write-up was no grounds for them to lock me up. Plus he "disapproved" the disciplinary against me. They wanted to see if I would blow (go off verbally) the night they placed me in Segregation but I didn't ...thanks to my teachings & technique I learned thru Vipassana. I must say, I really have grown and I am very much proud of myself. I just wished that these people will grow up as well.

Tell Bruce I said I haven't forgotten about him & all he's done for me. I hope he doesn't think that I've regressed any because he haven't heard from me. That's not the case. Being away from you guys makes it hard to relate to these people now. They look at me strange because of my practice, but hell I look at them differently because of their contentness about the way they are & their wishes to stay the same. Do you understand what I am saying? I hope so.

I guess I have kept you long enough. I must end here so I can turn the light off so my cell Partner can get some shut-eye, as well as me. It was 91 degrees outside today & the sun definately drained me dry. Take care of yourself my Dhamma sister.

Edward

Edward Johnson
September 5, 2004

My Dhamma Sister,

This last month has been difficult. It's been a test thru out this whole journey. To be tested in such a way that I have been,

I wouldn't wish it on anyone. And when you spoke about, you can hear Goenka's words, "Start again," I felt some joy in my heart. Because believe it or not, my Sister, I hear those words a lot in my head…just as I do his chanting. Goenka's wisdom is what I seek to obtain. He's such a brilliant man. One who has helped change the life of many. And one who's teaching of Dhamma has helped change mine (Life) for sure.

Well let me give you the scoop on what's been going on with me lately. There is a lot to explain too.

They have finally placed me on the Release list to go back to Population. I should be back in "Pop" by the time you receive my letter. I had sat with myself a week before the board (Segregation Board) met again. Your prior letter had done wonders. I had to sit and allow this solitude to become my Best Friend . . . in order to keep my peace within and to continue on that Peaceful Path that I found in 2002. That is a year I will never forget. I had found me again. It wasn't the "Gang" or Peer Pressure who helped me. It was a bunch of people who absolutely convinced me to deal with the truth. A bunch of people who I learned to love and trust. Those people are my family now. Those people are You, Bruce, Jonathan, Rick, Robin and all of my Dhamma Family. I will never go backwards my Sister . . . EVER!!! I will always start again.

See, the pressure at first was getting to me. That was because I was allowing it to. On Weds. (1st) at the Segregation Board I found myself still trying to explain the truth about what happened in the incident between me and the guy. When the Warden kept telling me he didn't believe me, I asked him to call the officer who wrote the disciplinary up and ask him. It just so happens, the officer was working "overtime" in segregation that day. So the Warden called him in and asked him; "Did he see the other guy spit in my face first before I hit him?" The officer responded by saying; "Yes!" Because of my past, people still tend to give me grief and want me to still be the person I once was inside of this jungle. Anyhow, the Warden released me to [general] population. I said "Thank you" and left out the room. I also thanked the officer for standing up and being truthful.

Jenny I look at these people and see so much corruption and Hate. I wished they all could just find or learn the teachings of Dhamma. They would definitely change the way they live and think. Maybe a lot of them doesn't want to change. I am just glad I have changed.

Today I went out on the exercise yard for 45 minutes and looked at the sun, the birds and just simply closed my eyes and breathe. I was really at Peace!

Jenny I am blessed and thankful to have you in my life. You've seen me cry and you've seen me smile and laugh. But most important, you've seen me change during the most trying times I have ever experienced in my life. I'm ready to get out of here (prison) and stay out. I want to share my experience nevertheless and teach the world or those who are willing to listen about the technique and the Peace that Dhamma has brought to my life. Now I can actually say, "I AM A MAN."

Take Care, my Dhamma Sister. And may Peace always be upon you.

With Lots of Metta,
Edward

Benjamin Oryang
September 18, 2004

Dear Jenny,

After over seven months, I am again reading a book titled: "The Moon Appears When the Water Is Still," by Ian McCrorie. It contains short reflections of which I would like to share one with you:

> Be thankful for all transgressions
> bestowed upon you by enemies or fate.
> Return every abuse with a smile,
> Pay for each insult with a gift.

A wonderful opportunity to practice
forgiveness and understanding has been gifted.
Only the hurt can hurt; only the angry can anger.
Who but those previously abused, abuse?

It is not the grace of God that keeps me from going there;
I am already there, one with my transgressor,
enmeshed in human misery.
But with thanks I choose not revenge but tolerence.
When the heart opens there are no strangers.

It is with that spirit that I write today, and also with the
hope that you are doing well. Love, greetings and peace. You
are in my heart.

Sincerely,
Benjamin Oryang

December 28, 2004 – January 1, 2005
Cell Course Rings in the New Year

*"On Monday December 27th, greatly moved by the magnitude of
horrific world EVENTS [the Pan-Asian tsunami], … I spoke about
my intention to do a 4-day course in my cell with the other two
prisoners I live with. I explained that this was serious work and
important to be done with certain understanding."*—John Johnson

John W. Johnson
December 28, 2004

Dear Bruce,

Greetings!
At midnight I will start my first Vipassana four-day course in
my cell. During this course I will practice with the technique
y'all brought with Dhamma teachings to Donaldson for us to
learn. We did learn too!
    *Will start with: Refuge in the triple gem—and the five
precepts—

*Will keep a strict schedule for meditation/with breaks

*Will cultivate sila (morality)—samadhi (concentration)
—pañña (wisdom)

*At end of day will read a couple of discourse summaries using the grey book—gift from Vipassana Research Publications.

*Will start with "anapanasati" (meditation on the breath) with "bala" (strength).

*Will eat breakfast only (raisin bran cereal/milk) in my cell. At evening will drink one tea without sweetner...

*Will cultivate metta and send metta through-out our suffering world.

*Will end this serious four-day course at midnight January 1st 2005.

In my cell are two people who are very willing to allow me to take part in this Vipassana Dhamma observation. 4 Block is now the worst cell-block at Donaldson. This is a wonderful opportunity...Bhavana-maya pañña...(experiential wisdom)

I understand that this letter may take time to get to you. Please tell everyone hello for me.

Metta, John
(old student) Donaldson Warrior

Bruce Stewart
January 29, 2005

Dear John,

Upon returning to Dhamma Dhara (Vipassana Meditation Centre) after conducting a course in Florida, I was delighted to receive your letter. I only wish I had time to respond sooner.

Both Jonathan and I were delighted to learn of your recent four-day self-course. We will be interested to hear how it went and if you (and possibly others) are planning future courses. We have had reports of several Donaldson Dhamma brothers sitting self courses . . . some did ten days. You're fortunate that you were able to have compatible cellmates who were willing to support you. This is their parami also.

Occasionally we hear news from some of you via Jenny, but we really appreciate news from you directly. Please let it be known that we are always delighted to hear from any of the Donaldson Dhamma Warriors and learn of their struggles and successes in Dhamma. In the meantime please pass on our warm regards and metta to all. The two Donaldson courses were truly historic and unique. My feeling is that, both individually and collectively, you all had such strong parami (virtues needed for liberation), otherwise Dhamma would surely have not come to such an unwholesome environment as Donaldson. On top of this, Goenkaji's remarkable visit was icing on the cake. Always remember, you all (sorry, y'all) have such a special place in our hearts and we think of you often with great warmth and best wishes for your continued growth in Dhamma. We admire and respect the gallant efforts so many of you made. No effort in Dhamma goes to waste!

2004 was quite a year for prison courses in the US. While we came close to having a women's course in Vermont, in the end they could not get enough students to make it happen. However, the new Vermont Department of Corrections Commissioner is now taking an interest and we hope to do a presentation to him soon. There's also interest in the Boston area and in California where I hear there is a Commissioner who is very program-orientated.

Last week Jonathan and I went to the United Nations where Tihar Jail's former Superintendent, Kiran Bedi (from the film "Doing Time, Doing Vipassana"), showed a documentary on Vipassana programs for the cadets at the India Police Training Academy where she is currently posted. I was on a panel and spoke of our Donaldson experience to an audience of about a hundred. The presentation drew much curiosity and interest and I'm confident good things will come from it. It was amazing to witness Vipassana being spoken about in such an important institution as the UN with such reverence and respect. Some wondered how Vipassana could be used at the UN.

We are curious if you get any support at all from the administration? Do any of you ever get to sit together? Now that you have been moved to a new block, do you ever get to see any of the other Dhamma brothers? Feel free to pass this letter around, or at least let them know we are thinking of them. I will leave you with this quote from the Sutta Nipata:

> "Lean in body, frugal in food, content with little and undisturbed, vain wishes gone and craving stilled, thus the desireless attain Nibbana (the ultimate unconditioned reality)."

As always, wishing you success for your continued growth in Dhamma.

Metta,
Bruce

John W. Johnson
January 19, 2005

Dearest Jenny,

Hey, I know you like hearing about the path at Donaldson and the "storm stories"—I have so many to tell you—very powerful dhammas here. Do not know where to start with such a wealth of experiences.

Maybe this—I just completed a four-day Vipassana course in 44 cell in the amazing 4-Block. Yes!!

On Monday December 27th, greatly moved by the magnitude of horrific world events, the intermixture of grasping aggregates at Donaldson . . . it became clear that to keep the torch of Dhamma alight . . . it was clear in my consciousness with a sense of transcendent awareness that I should take refuge with the triple gem: Buddha, Dhamma and Sangha (Community of Seekers).

The Four Noble Truths were and are deep-seated in my consciousness. It became clear that with a serious practice of the Noble Path it would be possible to cultivate Brahma Vihara (divine abodes) to all beings—right now . . . in my prison cell. Doing this at a time of great excitement—for the entire world—if not now? When? It rang in my heart like the sound of a Vipassana bell, to start again!!!

First, I spoke about my intention to do a 4-day course in my cell with the other two prisoners I live with. I explained that this was serious work and important to be done with certain understanding. I read and explained the reasons for sila (moral code). I explained that they could continue in the cell as they would during any other time. I explained what I would do during this course. I explained that this would not be easy for me, but I have a strong determination to practice. I read out loud to them, and to a couple of people who often come to visit, the story about the first Vipassana course at Donaldson (*Vipassana Newsletter* Vol. 29, No. 1, May 2002). I asked if they had any questions.

I placed on the wall next to a mirror in this cell the words of a "metta" (wishes for loving-kindness) that I would do for them, the world and myself. The "metta" sign I thought would be helpful if they also had an awareness contact with the words of volition that would be transmitted to all beings from our prison cell.

I also placed a sign for any other visitor to read about why I would not speak for four days.

I placed a reminder for my cell-mates of how they would help serve during the course, to please get ice twice a day for me and hot water once a day. You will find these enclosed:

I placed also in the cell two other signs with a few words of wisdom—to maybe aid their own thinking activity while I was working with my own discipline... You will see glue spots on the back of the paper. That is how I placed them on the wall of our prison cell. Maybe you will find another way to use these. I really am ready to allow the transmission of this metta and the Vipassana self-course to continue outward.

* REQUEST BY JOHN *

PLEASE FILL GREEN CUP WITH HOT WATER — FOR TEA —
ONE TIME IN THE MORNING ... AROUND 8:00 To 10:00 A.M.
— THANK YOU FOR YOUR SERVICE —

2ND REQUEST:

PLEASE FILL "TAN ICE MUG" WITH ICE TWICE —
*ONCE WHEN YOU GET HOT WATER FOR TEA — MORNING —
*ALSO, AROUND 10:00 P.M

THAT IS ALL I REQUEST,
— THANK YOU FOR YOUR SERVICE —

— WHY AM I DOING A SERIOUS MEDITATION RETREAT ?
THE BUDDHA ONCE SAID:

WHEN FACED WITH THE VICISSITUDES OF LIFE,
ONE'S MIND REMAINS UNSHAKEN,
SORROWLESS, STAINLESS, SECURE;
THIS IS THE GREATEST WELFARE.

YOU ARE YOUR OWN MASTER.
YOU MAKE YOUR OWN FUTURE
THEREFORE DISCIPLINE YOURSELF
AS A HORSE-DEALER TRAINS A THOROUGHBRED.

> Make an island of yourself,
> Make yourself your refuge; there is no other refuge.
> Make truth your island,
> Make truth your refuge; there is no other refuge.
> —*Maha-Parinibbana Sutta, Digha Nikaya, 16*

This was done as a reminder for me and to add a sense of understanding into the atmosphere of the surrounding influence of cell environment and the consciousness of anyone who read these signs while in the cell.

To be able to stay in the cell for the complete 96 hours was aided by the gift from my family during holiday package time. Raisin bran cereal with milk (powder) which I ate once a day. Each day I drank one cup of hot tea without sweetener.

This made it possible to meditate each day without hunger cravings or leaving the cell. For this opportunity I am greatly appreciative and have voiced this to my family deeply.

In my next letter I will share some of the experience of doing a Vipassana course in a prison cell. It is serious work and not to be taken lightly without a teacher. Will hold this for the next letter which I will mail Monday.

Just to sit to write this is not an easy task. Many distractions in a three-man cell in 4-Block. I do want to share some insight on each day of the course. To do this mindfully I will have to work at the letter during quiet times of the day.

Also, I will write Bruce again to let him know that it is possible to do a four-day Vipassana course in a cell at Donaldson. I am very grateful for the skills brought to us by y'all Northern Dhamma warriors.

> Metta,
> *John*

P.S. The four-day course started Wednesday Dec 29 12:01 a.m. and ended Jan. 1st Saturday at midnight. That means the metta you sent when writing your card to me was during the fourth day of the course. The metta was clear too on the fourth day!!

When the insight to do a self-course came into the "thinking activity" of my suffering mind it was a phenomenon that was beyond any expectations that I could have ever…ever imagined. This is very extraordinary contact with Dhamma. It is wonderful to know that, even in the mire of storm vicissitudes, Dhamma insight can still be teaching clarity of the way…the path of harmony with reality.

January 1 - August 10, 2005
Ups and Downs of Dhamma: Donaldson and Other Camps

"But to find serious practitioners of any kind of meditation . . . it appears as though we need to have a ongoing structured system that will stimulate—until we are able to be more self-reliant."— John Johnson

"Yes it has helped me to recognize the quality of my life and has in fact enhanced the quality of my life. It's like having a never ending

fountain where I can always quench my thirst. Or having a spring where I can be assured of having a place to be clean when I'm feeling soiled. It's all of that, and then some" —Charles X Ice

"It is almost impossible for me to get to the energy flow of meditation. It's noisy, very crowded. I can calm myself and regulate my breathing but that's about as far as I can go. I wish we had a Vipassana center here, because not only would daily meditation be improved but I know I need at least a ten day Vipassana every year!" —Grady Bankhead

"Being able to feel good about the moment you are in is one of the most difficult things to do in a maximum-security prison. Guess what though? Being able to connect with what's authentic about my existence, being able to forgive myself and being able to hold myself accountable for what I experience has enabled me to feel good about life, living and me—right now." —Omar Rahman

"I still get angry, but it doesn't last. I still get offended, but I'm quickly over it. I still experience depressed moments, yet only for moments. I've been blessed with awareness and with skills. Now instead of being caught up I recognize what is arising and I try to skillfully allow it to pass away, without attaching myself. "
—Omar Rahman

Leon Kennedy
January 3, 2005

To a dear & special friend: Mrs. Jenny Phillips

From someone who has no excuse for not writing: Mr. Leon Kennedy

Please forgive me for "soaring" past the normal salutations & greetings? But I'm really excited & so happy to be (finally) communicating w/you! I got your messages <u>each</u> time from Ms. Johnson.

As for myself, the journey has scenes of great joy, <u>pain</u> & many areas of growth & development.

Vipassana softened me, sensitized me. Although I continued to practice, I somehow managed to <u>create</u> personal problems in my marriage by re-acting improperly & thus imploding. (Long story, but you're familiar w/ the drill.) My heart as a result literally broke, my practice slowed, & soon my lack of coping skills led me to actually blaming (Vipassana) because of how sensitive & aware <u>emotionally</u> I had become. So I stopped.

But time changes things, I began to grow & let go of a lot of things, forgave myself & tried to move on. (Just carrying limited baggage now, J). Practice resumed, but mostly involving the scan, going directly to it. I then progressed & moved correctly to anna-panna—this is how I put myself to sleep "lots." I really utilize the technique to calm my mind/body in order to contemplate clearer the patterns of my life....this helps me to better find some balance in coping w/ my circumstances.

Yeah, I know we're not to mix the technique (I do indeed remember <u>all</u> that was taught to me by my teachers.) Yet Jenny, one has also to be mindful of environment, circumstances & those realities that come w/ it. In other words, "a brother has to try & survive w/what <u>works</u> for him." In regard to Vipassana & w/ all worthy respect, I can truly be grateful towards all that I learned. And yes, if they would ever let us do it again—I would leap at the chance, & I'd wait to serve again. That was the most sweet experience I've encountered other than my daughter's kisses & hugs. (Enclosed is a photo of her—she's 5 now, and loves her daddy very much; she also keeps me in line, has high expectations on her old man, makes me cry often (but not as much as she used to). O.B. & I still work together (thru—life's ups-n-downs...step by step) still best friends but don't tell em I said that, I'll deny it. I told James, Omar, O.B., John, Rick about the follow-up your doing. Hopefully my letter gave some assistance, I was honest. Thanx for being who you are & for caring, it makes the difference.

Mucho Metta,

Leon

James George
January 5, 2005

Dear Jenny,

I received your lovely card and was as always thrilled to hear
from you.

Jenny, as sad as it is to say, there are few who practice
meditation any more. Rick Smith sits with me at night. Rick
Alexander still meditates occasionally in the early mornings.
Other than this I honestly don't know anyone else who still
practices. I haven't seen John Johnson in several months but
wherever he is, I'm sure he still practices.

Jenny, the changes meditation has brought about in my life
are innumerable. I encountered feelings I never knew existed
when doing Vipassana, and since then I have learned to deal
with these feelings. The ability to love another human being
merely because they exist. To truly feel compassion for another.
I continue to grow daily in my recovery and my meditation
enables me to do this with candor. I now embrace each new day
with enthusiasm, anxious to see what God has planned for me
today.

I took your card over to Ms. Johnson [in drug treatment]
and she told me you are planning to visit us next month. This
is wonderful news and I am anxious to see you and Robin
again.

I will close for now so know we miss you and will be very
pleased when we see you. Hope to hear from you soon.

Much Metta, *James*

Benjamin Oryang
January 6, 2005

Dear Jenny,

HAPPY NEW YEAR!!!

Things on this end have been fast-paced for me despite
the one month break from the usual classes; otherwise I am
well under the circumstances. Next week marks the start of
the regular programs for the year—beginning with Houses of
Healing on Monday—so I am currently in the process of trying
to shift gears from an untamed schedule which developed over
the past month.

The block where I live (One-Block) has been—is being—
transformed into the "New Beginner's" program and it has
been quite chaotic with technicalities. The residents voted
me in as one of the three regents whose duty it is to establish
an agenda and goals for the ninety-six men involved in the
program. I initially wanted to decline but after a little prodding
accepted the position. That decision has been the cause of
much stress over the past several weeks. Of course things are
beginning to settle down now and get better, and I intend to
step down from the position as soon as the program is fully on
its own feet—hopefully within the next month or so.

There is a lot of room for improvement in my meditation
practice. Though one's practice is a personal thing, it is an even
greater challenge to continue without the benefit of regular
group sittings. Lately I have not kept a regular schedule of
sitting but I am always encouraged by John, Omar and some
of our other Dhamma brothers through their commitment.
Especially John, who always shares so much with us about his
experiences. We still meet every Wednesday under the auspices
of another scheduled class in the "group room," and that gives
us the opportunity to share our bond with each other. Every
now-and-then we even get the chance to sneak in a Goenkaji
CD and sit for about an hour with his instructions. I wonder
what would happen if we were caught.

My friend Troy has been away from here for a few weeks
now, and I miss him dearly. We are all hoping that things with
the court are working out well for him.

My father recently sent me a letter in which he says his
health is satisfactory. The last report he gave was that the
cancer was under control with the periodic use of chemo-

therapy. He hasn't voiced any immediate plans of returning to the U.S. to visit, but David [my brother] may be visiting Uganda within the next few months or so.

The tsunami has been devastating. Just a few weeks ago most people had no idea what one was. It is undoubtedly the most wide spread and deadly natural disaster of our times. My heart and much metta go out to all who have been affected by it.

You are in my heart Jenny. I will let you know how things go with the Houses of Healing class and the others next week. Greetings from Wayne Finch.

Metta, OB

John W. Johnson
March 9, 2005

Dear Bruce,

Great letter with visuals . . . you really gave a passageway for me to seek out the other Dhamma Brothers. For the past seven months I have only seen a few. Some also live in my block area. With your letter in hand I was successful at moving around other parts of Donaldson. This has been an opportunity to touch base and let them be conscious of our relationship with Dhamma and each other.

Thank you for bringing a way to do this. When you said "feel free" to pass this letter around . . . you inspired me.

One of the most interesting responses came from Jimmy Blackmon (free-world drug counselor—first group who came to Shelburne). He picked right up with the quote from Sutta Nipata. This really brought happiness to me, for I too recognize the clear Dhamma insight within that quote. He stated the impact that the course had on him and still does in a subtle way.

Another person who took the course at Donaldson who is part of the drug dorm . . . read your letter, and I watched his attention go from that . . . to asking me if I knew of anyone who lives in the blocks—that might want to buy a set of dice!! This happens all the time—with the habitual process of the convict mind—I just try to be non-judgmental. Not easy at times.

In your letter you asked if "I or we" get any support from the administration at all. Can't say we do. Bruce, for the past few years I have really worked at not being a "seeker of control." Kind of a middle-way to see what would arise. For me this took a lot of emptying my rebellious nature.

I have always felt that "if" the administration would see serious practitioners of meditation—that minds would change. Really, I think that the administration would rather see "chaos with vain superstition," because this is familiar and does not shake their false zone of comfort.

But to find serious practitioners of any kind of meditation . . . it appears as though we need to have a ongoing structured system that will stimulate—until we are able to be more self-reliant.

For me—I am making an effort to move out of the cell-block housing. Too much mental illness in this part of the prison and too much cigarette secondhand smoke. This block experience was good for me, a humbling opportunity and I also was able to do a four-day self-course. Time to move on, though.

I see the Drug Dorm as a possible right effort. This location is a place where other prisoners are living with a structured system to remove addictions and also have a concentration of Vipassana old students. I see a possible way that my own effort of practice may allow others to join in with group meditation.

In your letter you mentioned other Dhamma warriors with self-courses... some did ten-days. I have no idea who they are. I will not ask. What I will continue to do is to pass your letter around and let arise what arises to be natural.

Within the next week I should know if I am able to move to Drug Dorm Housing. Will write you about the environment and then I will be able to relate to your question about future self courses, etc.

Good to hear that you are doing courses in Florida. I really like that part of Northern Florida. Very happy to hear about the plans for a Vipassana center there.

John

Grady Bankhead
March 13, 2005

Dear Jenny

As I wrote in my last letter or at least I meant to – no funds, no visits, no phone calls, nothing for so long now that I've adjusted to it. You know old folks like me sometimes forget whether we did something or not. Things have been really hard for me for quite a while and as we both know things may or may not get any better.

Yes, I meditate every day and I only use the Vipassana technique. But I have to say just doing the meditation for an hour or so a day makes it really hard and most often impossible to get any further than anapana. I know I should do more.

Jenny so many people write about their cases and the childhood that led to it that I think I'd like to do something different. I'd like to write about all the doors that have opened up for me through the love of others I meet in here and the doors opened through the education I've received during the last 19 years. I'm so far from the person I was back then that maybe some folks would like to hear how the transition took place.

Metta, *Grady*

Charles Ice
March 31, 2005

May Peace be unto you:

Dear Jenny,

My financial situation has deteriorated but it should be getting better once I receive my first pay-check from the industrial department in another month or so.

Yes, it was a very big surprise to see Ed when I got here. Only problem is that this institution is very restrictive, so we're not able to sit together. We have spoken to each other about our experiences and how we would like to go through another course.

My meditation practice has affected my life in different ways. Sometimes, I am so peaceful, I am thought to be weak. And that poses many problems in this world of vultures. But sometimes I'm boiling inside from trying to cope with my situation. I appreciate being in this demanding and volatile environment, because I've learned that struggle is ordained. Each time I go through a troubled situation, I then experience the ease of knowing how to handle this type of situation the next time it arises. So, yes, meditation has helped me to find inner-peace. Mostly because I'm now more comfortable with my being in my own person. Meditation has helped me gain self-acceptance, where I don't need other people's opinions to validate my existence.

So, yes it has helped me to recognize the quality of my life and has in fact enhanced the quality of my life. It's like having a never ending fountain where I can always quench my thirst. Or having a spring where I can be assured of having a place to be clean when I'm feeling soiled. It's all of that, and then some. I'm forever grateful to you, Robin, Dr. Marshall and Goenkaji for exposing me to whole new world and making it possible for me and everyone else who was allowed to experience Vipassana to experience what we never experienced before. Thank You! Much Metta to you and the whole Dhamma center!

Charles X Ice

Charles Ice
May 8, 2005

May Peace Be Unto You:

Dear Jenny,

Thank you for writing that my letter was an extraordinary
one. I was only sharing my thoughts with you, I didn't think of
it as something special.

Thank You! for staying in touch. Most times when someone
says that to an incarcerated person, it's never acted on.

The "trouble situations" are times when the closed in area,
filled with a lot of different attitudes and mindsets, become
volatile. There's this one situation where a "young" man got
behind me in a line to come in from trade school. He got so
close, he was breathing down my neck and his toes were on my
heels.

I "respectfully" informed him that he was too close. His
response was that he wasn't a homosexual and that his father
didn't raise a punk. I then let him know that because I couldn't
read his thoughts, his actions were the [only] evidence of how
he thinks. He says "I will respect any man." When I showed
him by explanation that he was disrespecting me at that precise
moment, he got angry and wanted to fight saying that I was
accusing him of being gay. He didn't stop to think that in
prison there are some minds that thought that way, having an
attraction towards another man. And that by his actions in this
situation was indicative that he may have thought like that. I
was not able to control my own anger at that point so when he
issued the challenge I accepted it and punched him out. We
talked after the incident, and because hindsight is 100%, we
both recognized our errors in how we handled the situation.

The latest situation that got me transferred to St. Clair happened when the maintenance crew was painting the beds that
day. They painted one whole side the previous day. It was when
I asked a guy if he would mind if we used his bed to hold the

property of the guy whose bed he had used to hold his stuff on while his bed was being painted the previous day. At first, the guy acted as though he didn't know who I was talking about. When I described for him that it was the same person whose bed he used yesterday, he starts cursing me out saying he's tired of me watching him. He's upstairs on the tier while he's doing all of this, so I ask him to just stay up there with all that. I tried being diplomatic but he wasn't hearing me. So I gave him a choice. He could pursue his present course and wind up sending me to Segregation and himself to the infirmary. I thought he got the message, but as I was completing placing my belongings on someone else's bed, he comes downstairs and gets in my face and blocks my attempts to get by him. So, I lightly placed the back of my hand on his chest and attempted to go around him. He took a swing at me, one I anticipated, so I counter-punched him and knocked him out. I look back on that and I wonder what I could've done better to avoid the altercation. Of course, there are even a hundred different scenarios that play out in my mind.

I think that if I never place myself in these situations I would not have had to deal with them. I could step out of any situation as soon as it becomes an aggressive one. I realize that now. I'm always looking for ways to improve myself. I'll be forever indebted to you, Bruce, Jonathan, Dr. Marshall and Goenkaji for making it possible for the Vipassana program to come into Donaldson. Because of that program, I can observe circumstances, situations and events more fully, thereby allowing me to maneuver through life in a more peaceful way. That's because I'm learning the inner me and what stimuli is most potent in making me respond.

I'll end this letter right here for now with a whole lot of Metta! Much Metta! To you!

Your friend in Dhamma,
Charles X Ice.

May Peace, Blessings and much metta be bestowed upon you, eternally!

Charles Ice
(no date, *continued*)

Dear Jenny,

Me? I'm doing well, considering the circumstances. Aneecha!
(Impermanence!)

I'm very honored that something that I've written has had
such an impact on you. And yes, you are correct when you
write that it seems I am learning about myself and applying
what I've learned to a very challenging environment. I've
always been able to express myself much better on paper than
I can orally. I suppose it has to do with being able to think
objectively before writing what I think. Having the chance to
collect my thoughts then putting them on paper helps alot.

I strive to be honest in thoughts, deed and actions so that
my word can mean something. And because I feel close to you,
I have no problem being open and frank about my situation.

Yes, Jenny, I believe we always have choices no matter what
the situation. We don't always choose the proper course, but
we choose nevertheless. Even in our improper choices there
is a lesson learned, or should be learned anyway. Even when
we can walk away from an instance that has the potential to
get volatile, we <u>choose</u> to walk away. When we don't choose to
walk away, we choose not to. But the option is always there for
us to take. Although it's simpler to walk away and stay peaceful, it may be confused with cowardice or weakness. Then, the
simple thing becomes a greater burden when the one we walk
away from chooses to press the issue even further. In the Holy
Qur'an, it says to: "meet a force with equal force." "And to fight
with those who fight with you. But if they turn away then fight
them not."

Some people are just bullies at heart, and they will forever
remain so unless they're taught that it is wise not to be so.
That only happens when they run across someone who cares
enough about them to stop them from behaving poorly.

I wish the Vipassana program was more active for we who have been through the program. It feels like I've left something undone or incomplete. I long for the chance to do a sitting at one of the Dhamma centers. I really want to be free! This constricted environment weighs heavy on my very soul and spirit. Aneecha! Right!

I'm going to close this letter right here for now with a promise to write more soon.

Peace and Metta, *Charles X Ice*

Grady Bankhead
April 10, 2005

Dear Jenny,

Jenny my days are really hard. When I wake up I have to try and figure out where I'm gonna be able to get a cup of coffee. If they don't have anything edible in the chow hall then I have to find something to eat. I don't have any money so I don't get to draw from the store. Even stamps are hard for me to come up with. There's no jobs here where you earn any money. So my point is life every day is a real struggle for me.

It is almost impossible for me to get to the energy flow of meditation. It's noisy, very crowded. I can calm myself and regulate my breathing but that's about as far as I can go. I wish we had a Vipassana center here, because not only would daily meditation be improved but I know I need at least a ten day Vipassana every year!

I think I will just write my story; it's just like everything else right now for me. It's got to be put second in priorities be cause just everyday getting by has to come first.

When you don't have anything, cosmetics, clothes, shoes, food to eat or drink, your time is consumed with getting those things. What the state gives you is the absolute worst of everything.

Lots of Metta, *Grady*

John W. Johnson
April 10, 2005

Dear Bruce,

Good news!!

I am now living in the Drug Dorm at Donaldson. It is very interesting because of the nature of the dorm—a rehabilitation environment for people with addictions. This is going to be a very powerful place for me to practice. It is wise, I think, that I waited until this time of my practice to attempt to live in such an environment. Each part of Donaldson has different forms of Dhammas that effect the environment and the lives of the people who inhabit there. Kind of different cultures of people who have picked up its uniqueness of each area of doing time. It is odd thinking, but real.

Bruce—I had a very remarkable visit last week with a human rights attorney. She is out of Georgia and working on some issues of prison reform. As you may remember I am an activist for prison reform.

This was the original purpose of the visit . . . to investigate possible future litigation. Our conversation exchange went toward how it is possible for prisoners to find reform while doing time—even in an Alabama prison system.

I spoke about being a Vipassana practioner. She was very interested to hear about my experience. In fact she was amazed to hear that I had taken part in two courses and even a four-day self-course in my cell.

As it turned out, I too was amazed to hear that an associate in her firm was a new student of Vipassana who had recently taken two courses and recently married a Vipassana practioner. She spoke about how they were very faithful at doing Vipassana twice a day—even in a motel room while on the road for business.

This attorney said she did not think she could take the course—because she said that her patience would not allow her to take the course because she could not sit for nine days — I said it was ten days and that she could do it!! And that her whole life would be rich with improvement. Her relationships would be much more harmonious and that a positive transformation would be realized. She said that I had convinced her to take a course with her colleague. Bruce, who would've ever thought that two years after taking this course . . . that a free-world attorney would visit me and be inspired to do Vipassana because of a talk with me at Donaldson?

As you said, "No effort in Dhamma goes to waste!" Very true, very true.

Here is another point of interest. The "F-Dorm" is the first dorm I ever started to meditate in. Each morning I meditate in a location where I first attempted to learn about meditation. Now I do Vipassana in that same area . . . I am very grateful.

Will write you about some of my "realizing change" while being a part of the drug program. It is not a easy program. I am gaining a huge amount of personal insight with the aid of doing the Rehabilitation Drug Program with a Vipassana practice each day. Powerful Dhamma flowing.

Metta to all ya'll, *John*

Willie Carroll
April 27. 2005

"Vipassana For Me"

Having done almost 23½ years in the Alabama Prison system—where each day I've lived not wanting to die but aware that my behavior was in fact a death sentence. I wanted rehabilitation over a whole lot of defects in my life. My attitude for one, my sense of respect for others was low—even though I sincerely believed in God—I still didn't have what I needed to live peacefully regardless of conditions—(prison). I sought the help of Dr. Ron Cavanaugh who offered Mental Health classes along with Dr. Marshall. These classes offered me information that led me into drug treatment. I entered the Crime Bill Program around 1998 and has been involved since that time.

I was invited to watch a Vipassana film shot over in one of the units in Drug treatment [Changing from Inside, actually filmed at NRF, Seattle]. Seeing the spiritual enchantment on lost souls such as I—crying and smiling—really brought a ray of hope within me—it also made me want to experience Vipassana.

In 2002 of May—I along with eighteen other prisoners— met Jenny, Rick, Bruce, and Jonathan—we (prisoners) was interviewed—we agreed to take on ten days of total silence in a gym here at the prison. At first I was feeling a little fear—I was scared for real. Day one, I spent trying to relax and get some inner strength together to avoid quitting. Day two was the same—Day three, I drifted back into my beginnings—child- hood, teenage times—all that I'd avoided thinking of refused to go away—I even tried to dream—my thoughts refused to play the game I wanted it to play—this was going to happen no matter what. I was going to see me, deal with me, no matter what. Day four and five was spent in so much pain. My body sweated—my spirit became broken. I found myself seeking to be forgiven; my only desire was to have God help me away from so many painful memories. Meditating day in and out in seclusion—was something like standing before God telling him everything I'd done, and genuinely being sorry for it. All my past surfaced—the guilt—the shame, the love, the moments of anger—At times I really needed to talk to Jonathan or Bruce because I felt burdened so heavy that I'd break my silence.

Though having people there for me to reach out to—nev- ertheless—I was alone. Day six, having learned to manage and accept my emotions for what they really was—I gained strength to face myself and to learn more of myself. Never before had I ever experienced anything like this. I'm still deeply impressed by Vipassana…My remaining days—seven to ten—I spent meditating—rehabilitating my total being. I entered Day one with an attitude of Superman and left feeling free—but afraid of hearing my past confront me. However, I've learned to work Vipassana meditation daily—it provides me serenity at the beginning and ending of my day. I've learned to greet life on simpler terms. Being an addict of drug

usage—a "Recovery"ing Addict—with the twelve step program
and practicing the teachings of meditation—I'm able to pray
better—see Life better—and to Love Life on a higher level of
respect—In all aspects...my experience I can't explain enough
to anyone—other than to say—I truly value that experience
more than any ever that I've experienced before.

"The difference Vipassana has given me"

First off—taking the ten-day course was a great step taken
for me. Never before had I attempted to become a particpant
in any meditation—especially not for ten days of total silence.
Before entering the course, I could barely put up with anybody
else's attitude different from mines. To get my point across in
my ill attempts for a solution if words couldn't find peace, I'd
force fights. Vipassana has provided me with the tool to endure
a whole lot and then some. I can now talk to the worse of
attitudes and still keep my composure—I can now be human to
myself and others. I'm not cured of my lack of knowledge but
this experience has allowed me room to grow and to respect
my growth. "No matter where I go, there I am," is one of the
most profound discoveries about my being that I'll ever realize.
Never will I forget what I went through in those ten days—the
teachings nor the pain of learning will I ever forget.

The experience was a very rewarding blessing that no
words can express. The changes within me I witness daily in
my dealings with others and myself. And they're appreciated
deeply—the difference Vipassana made was life instead of death
to a dying man.

Willie Carroll Jr.

Omar Rahman
May 26, 2005

Dear Jenny,

I feel as potent as the landscape imagery of Maxfield
Parrish's "June Skies." Remember the last card you sent me?
Well I'm running five miles five days a week under these June
skies and I'm physically brimming. But what I'm raving about
is my new found emotional potency that's rising.

Jenny being able to feel good about the moment you are in
is one of the most difficult things to do in a maximum-security
prison. Guess what though? Being able to connect with what's
authentic about my existence, being able to forgive myself and
being able to hold myself accountable for what I experience
has enabled me to feel good about life, living and me—right
now. In this maximum-security prison. The reason this is big
stuff for me is because for about ten years of my incarceration I
couldn't smell the morning dew on the grass in the spring. For
me there is a feeling that goes with this experience that began
when I was a child. I no longer had the feeling that went with
certain experience Jenny. It felt as if I was missing something
and it generated a subtle grief that I didn't understand. These
years were the hardest and most difficult years of my life.

Guess what though! I've come through that phase of my
growth and learning. Yes! Fifty-two and still growing. Let me
tell you Jenny, morning dew in the spring never smelled better.
I still get angry, but it doesn't last. I still get offended, but I'm
quickly over it. I still experience depressed moments, yet only
for moments. I've been blessed with awareness and with skills.
Now instead of being caught up I recognize what is arising and
I skillfully, or I try to skillfully, allow it to pass away without
attaching myself.

This is good stuff for me, especially where I am. I mean if
you have spent 23 years in Alabama's prison system, there is
nothing better that can happen to you than what has happened
to me.

Jenny for the past several years my life has been a large upheaval. An ongoing one. Something akin to what the farmer does when he wants to bring new life out of the Earth. A breaking of ground if you will.

In the commercial industry there is a concept called "disruptive technology." These are new technologies that change the way things have traditionally been done. In most cases even causing age old institutions to change to remain competitive. One thing that comes to mind, for example, is the use of the internet to handle telephone calls.

Well, I want to borrow this concept to apply to experiences we can have and people we can meet. Can we call them "disruptive experiences" or "disruptive people;" people who bring experiences and information into your life that break you out of life-robbing mental and emotional constructs and introduce more authentic ways of being. Well, then, you, Robin, Bruce, Jonathan and Rick are who I call that disruptive group of people in my life. Thank you all so much for disrupting me from my inertia because I was going nowhere. Now it seems I'm all over the place. These past several years have been one big ramp of a learning curve. And that's what I mean about my life being an upheaval.

Guess what! More good stuff been coming out of the ground of me than I can remember. I feel good about being generous and kind, and how I manage my inner experiences.

Speaking of upheavals we could use a cultural one in this State, Jenny. This state is so hide-bound to a narcissistic view of reality and human affairs. There's this seemingly juvenile groping of self that permeates the decision-making process here. We still march to the palpitations of past prides and prejudices here. Progress here is a backward looking affair and change is a slow moving train that never seems to stay moving long enough to get anywhere.

I do apologize for the lack of meaningful and intelligent responsiveness you all encounter from people of this state. Those of us who have been able to rise above the inertia of ignorance that this state languishes in are grateful and appreciative to you all for showing us how to lift ourselves up.

Metta to You all,
Omar

Benjamin Oryang
June 12, 2005

Dear Jenny,

It has been raining quite abit over the past 24 hours due to tropical storm "Arlene." In my block there are at least thirty plastic-gallon containers which have been strategically positioned in the dayroom to catch dripping water from the leaky roof. About six of the leaking areas are new, but that could be expected in light of the heavy-consistent shower.

Due to some delays we will not be starting the Houses of Healing classes until tomorrow afternoon, and I'm looking forward to that. And yes, it would be very helpful if we had some more books. Over the past two years we have required that the guys use the books while attending the course, and then return them for use by the next group of students. As would be expected, we still lose quite a few of them—so it will be a big help to have some.

Last week Omar, John, Milton, Leon and I were the only people to show up for a New Solution's class, so we had a group sitting—using one of Goenkaji's C.D.s—for an hour. It felt as though we were stealing something, but we all decided to go through with it anyway. We plan to sit again whenever such an opportunity presents itself, irrespective of any repurcussions. We are also in the process of developing a strategy for civil action to challenge the Department of Corrections' unfairness towards meditators like ourselves.

Otherwise, we are doing okay under the circumstances.

Greetings from all over here. You are in my heart, Jenny.

OB

Edward Johnson
July 18, 2005

Dear Jenny,

Thanks, my friend, for being there for me and for believing in me. And also for not giving up on me—even when at times I lose focus. All because I allow these people to enter inside my circumference. That's my fault!! Because if I was staying the course like I'm suppose to then they wouldn't have that opportunity to enter my comfort zone.

My sister your words scares me. It's like being a part of someone's thoughts and heart. Everything you wrote is/was true. I have been getting a li'l despair about my situation. Nevertheless I still be trying my best to get back on course. Seeing your face again along with other people who cares . . . who Really Really cares about the person I've become, makes me feel a sense of Relief.

Jenny this letter has been a long time coming. I just be scared. Because like you said I feel as though I have let a lot of people down and am very disappointed with myself. However I refuse to continue to stay the negative course that these people want me to. I am going to get back on the course that I have grown to love and the course that has taught me more than these people could ever teach me. The teachings of Dhamma is the Peace I need and want.

My sister, I just came out of three-day sitting with myself. I couldn't believe these guys respected my space. I told my cell partner that I am about to meditate for three days and will he give me that much respect and Space. He said, "Yes." So I went for it. And, my sister, it helped me so much. To practice like that in this hostile environment really is hard. But I made it work. It was real lovely.

I haven't had the opportunity to "sit" with "Ice" yet. He's doing well and seems to be at Peace. I like that. We talk every chance we get. He helps me out a lot. And I do mean a lot. Both of us are struggling but we will make it. I'm no fool nor am I stupid. I know without the teachings of Dhamma I still will be on a path of Destruction. There is so much I wanna reveal to the world about the profound truth of Dhamma.

I haven't spoken to momma this week. I have been having problems financially and haven't been able to catch the Store and get the things I need. Momma has been struggling as well. So that kind of bother me. Especially with the fact that I hate to depend on anyone because I hate to be let down. Right now I am just living on the Land. Meaning: borrowing food, etc., from guys that is okay with me.

My sister, I am going to close now.
Edward

Rick Smith
July 21, 2005

Dear Jenny,

Greetings in the spirit of Vipassana! Ms. Johnson told me in her office the other day that you would like to hear from me and the rest of the Dhamma family here in the Deep South. So . . . here I am. From what Ms. J. had to say—you are interested to know some questions concerning the affects of Vipassana on my life.

Jenny, I meditate twice a day for one hour—I don't always use the Vipassana technique though—as you are aware—I practiced meditation before Vipassana—in fact, I have 21 years or more in it now. Also—I have been in treatment all that time—so I am not a good clinical candidate.

The benefits I gain from meditation are many faceted. I have some serious peace of mind. I am able to focus on goals and projects with laser like intensity. Also in relationships I feel more honest with the people I love and care for and I have a sense of humor about life that I don't think would be there if it weren't for the quiet time.

You can basically tell how much growth you experience by the hunger you have to "sit" daily. I look forward to my quiet time with God/universe/Love/Life with joyous expectance of a lover on a distant shore. Every day is new to me. I've had one heck of a year (January). It started with the "appearance" of negativity—(Lock-up) of course it was "bullshit"—but I was centered immediately and was looking for the highest version of the experience and was able to make contact with it and I feel that the practice of meditation has had a lot to do with that.

I have the biggest blessings of all in my relationships—I am so fortunate to share my life with Amazing friends out there such as yourself and the men in here I cherish.

The Spiritual event of Right Living, Right thought . . . I hold onto what works. Meditation works. I am proof of that daily.

Jenny, Take Care—Be blessed!
Much Metta, and Namasté, *Rick*

James George
August 10, 2005

Dear Jenny,

I'm sure you have heard about [the two Dhamma Brothers] by now and some of what they have been going through [accused of drug use].

This is what happens when we lose focus on who we are, where we are at and how we got here. Our recovery must remain paramount in our mind and I firmly believe that had they continued to practice their meditation daily, they probably would not have slipped.

The ripple effect of their actions are still being felt through-out the program. Not just the end result and their being moved out but what led up to it. The program suffered from their actions and this hurt me. This may sound corny, but Jenny, this program means the world to me and it breaks my heart to see it deteriorate the way it has over the last couple years. This program literally pulled me from the gates of hell. That's just how serious my addiction had become. I didn't care about anyone or anything, only where I was going to get my next high.

Now my life has purpose and direction. Now I not only care about myself, which I didn't before, but now I genuinely care about others. True enough, I have been denied any relief by the courts, and for a brief moment I fell into melancholy. However, I thank God I didn't use [drugs], which I would have a few short years ago. In fact, I can honestly say the thought never even entered my mind. What I did was get still and focused, and let it pass. All things are impermanent....

I do worry about Tracey as her health isn't the best, and it's really difficult for her to make it on that meager stipend she receives from the government. But she is hanging in there and I love her for that.

Well, I guess I'll close for now so take care. Rick Smith sends his regards as well as John Johnson.

Much Metta,
James

Timeless (2004 - 2006)
Life and Death: Dhamma Brothers Lose Loved Ones

"The last time I saw Brandy was when she was three at her adoption hearing. . .She found me about four years ago. I know she loved me & and I know she knew I loved her."—Grady Bankhead

"As to more pleasant things, still meditating. It really helped me to stay calm through all that has happened...So I'm surviving. Of course I'd love to have someone outside of here to share things with but as of now there's no one and I guess that's really all right for now. It doesn't cause the sadness that I used to feel."
—Grady Bankhead

"The past weeks were, indeed, filled with a lot of pain and the feelings of loss. 'Maranam pi dukkham' (the arising of death causes more suffering)—the Buddha's words are true."—OB Oryang

"I buried the emotional grief of my mother passing so deep and so quick that I've never felt anything. I kept piling stuff on top of my grief until death became my friend and I completely lost all to death—it was just something that happened. I'd locked myself in a prison worse than any other. Anyway, I'm finally able to grieve over my mother's death and not be ashamed."—Johnny Mack Young

Benjamin Oryang
January 10, 2004 *(continued)*

Dear Jenny,

Just before sitting down to write this letter, I found out that my mother had been admitted into hospital pending gall bladder surgery. The operation is scheduled for Monday the 12th, by which time it is hoped that she will be stable enough for the procedure. For reasons unbeknownst to me and for the first time ever upon hearing such news, I am not panicked or jumpy. In the same token, I am far from being indifferent to the situation. I wonder if this calm will be short-lived. Anyhow, I will keep you informed as to Mum's condition.

OB

Benjamin Oryang
March 22, 2004

Dear Jenny,

Just a quick note to inform you that my mother passed away last Wednesday. I am doing okay, though I don't know where or how to proceed from here. She was my reason for virtually everything. It is going to be very difficult.

Otherwise, I am coping. The family is getting a lot of support from several relatives and friends. My job will now be to try and keep us all united since the backbone of the family is no longer physically present with us.

This is just a short note for now, but I will keep in touch. Please send me metta.

You are in my heart—*OB*

Benjamin Oryang
April 22, 2004

Dear Jonathan,

Thank you so much for writing. The past weeks were, indeed, filled with a lot of pain and the feelings of loss. *"Maranam pi dukkham"* (the arising of death causes more suffering)—the Buddha's words are true.

Otherwise, with thanks for a lot of support and metta from friends like you, Jenny and Bruce, I am coping. I am not even going to attempt to reconcile with the loss, but will try to adjust to it instead. You know, losing my mother had constituted my biggest fear in the preceding few years. Now a whole new world is open which, though still quite foreign, will in due time start to get clearer.

The past month has seen me in a struggle with the meditation process, but I know that the difficulties are—like their cause—impermanent. They will pass. They will arise again, and then pass again. My job is to continue the practice, irrespective of the attendant circumstances, and that is what I intend to do.

Metta,
OB

Grady Bankhead
February 14, 2005

Dear Jenny,

I know it's been a long time since you heard from me. I've meant to write several times, and I don't know why I haven't. Hope you know just because I haven't wrote doesn't mean that you are forgotten because that could never happen.

In the time that you haven't heard from me, life & death has gone on. I've had the rest of my family members pass away. My daughter Brandy in Mobile was murdered. I know how it feels on both sides now. One thing it did do was confirm my beliefs on capital punishment and excessive stays in prison. I haven't been nor am I now angry with the man that did it. So many people getting killed every day, it's a wonder that it hasn't touched myself or a loved one before now. When it happened, I was raw inside for a week or so and as it eased I was able to talk about it. So I'm okay -----

As to more pleasant things, still meditating. It really helped me to stay calm through all that has happened...So I'm surviving. Of course I'd love to have someone outside of here to share things with but as of now there's no one and I guess that's really all right for now. It doesn't cause the sadness that I used to feel.

I have friends in here that are like family to me and some that care that are out of here of which of course you're included.

So I guess I have caught you up to date and I just keep trucking on but with a lot more calm in my life.

Hope to hear from you. Take care.

With love, *Grady*

P.S. Happy Valentine's Day

Grady Bankhead
March 31, 2005 *(continued)*

Dear Jenny,

Thank you for your card. It was really nice to hear from you.
I was so shocked to receive mail. I don't even go to mail call
any more so I didn't hear my name called. About 3 guys came
to tell me I had mail. I guess it surprised them as much as it
did myself. So aside from it being great to hear from you, it
also created some fun.

Brandy was 29, and had four children who are beautiful.
My nickname for her was Fireball because of her red hair. I
may have told you a story of the only time in my life when I
thought I did the right thing. Which was to allow Brandy to be
adopted by her mother and new husband. Anyway the last time
I saw Brandy was when she was 3 at her adoption hearing. She
ran across the courtroom, grabbed my leg, and yelled, "Daddy!
Daddy!" It broke my heart. I still thought I was doing the right
thing. Brandy wrote about twice a year and I talked to her once
on the phone. She found me about four years ago. I know she
loved me & and I know she knew I loved her.

Its just too many loved ones are gone from my life. There's
no one left to hear from. I haven't had a visit in three years.

I'm gonna close for now. Let me know what you are up to.

Metta, *Grady*

Johnny M. Young
February 9, 2006

Dear Jenny,

It is my prayer that you, family, loved ones are enjoying a
Blessed health. As for myself, I'm Blessed with the gift of life
and that is enough for me, especially since I'll be fifty-seven
years on the Earth March 11th.

Mrs. Johnson informed me that she had heard from you and I really want to share a unique experience with you and desire to hear your opinion—if any.

I was watching Mrs. Martin Luther King's funeral and when her daughter Bernice spoke over her casket, a resident setting next to me asked what was wrong. It was only then that I noticed tears freely flowing down my cheeks. I told him that since I've been taking this class MAKING PEACE WITH YOUR PAST, I've become overly sensitive. I also told him that I was a little concerned over his sudden sense of empathy. Being in treatment over six years, I've acquired tools to dissect my behavior and recognized the tears as the product of emotional sickness.

I meditated for three plus hours and went deeper into myself than ever before. I experienced a vision where it was not Bernice standing in front of the casket but me. It was not Mrs. King in the casket but my mother. I couldn't stop the tears and had to stop my meditation.

I first went to prison in 1965 when I was fifteen years of age with a three-year sentence, during which I'd gotten stabbed twice and had stabbed seven people. I'd turned into a hard-core man-child in a violent world where a show of any sign of weakness and you became a victim.

My mother died in 1968, a couple of months before my release. I was allowed to go to the funeral, hands cuffed behind my back and legs shackled, with two white prison guards. The Alabama prison system was still racially segregated at the time and there were no blacks working in such positions. If they had been allowed such jobs they would have had to guard white prisoners and that just wasn't going to happen in the segregated south.

There I stood in front of the casket, looking at my mothers unsmiling face in an all Black church with two white guards standing behind me. I didn't know at the time, but it was anger that allowed me to show no emotions, only bitterness. As the years passed, I buried the emotional grief of my mother passing so deep and so quick that I've never felt anything. I kept piling stuff on top of my grief until death became my friend and I completely lost all to death—it was just something that happened. I'd locked myself in a prison worse than any other.

Anyway, I'm finally able to grieve over my mother's death and not be ashamed. I still have to remember "stuff" and deal with it, but I can say that I'm now equipped to deal my "stuff." We shall speak more of emotional healing and the adult child when next I see you.

Sorry about the length of this letter, but you know we prisoners can be long winded at times when it comes to letter writing.

Yours,

Johnny Mack

January 2006
Legal Again: Vipassana Reinstated
A Three-Day Course in the Gym

"The whole universe… is in alignment for 'vipassana' at Donaldson—again."—John Johnson

"I know Vipassana can make a significant impact on the system if only it is embraced. The change in the thinking of the inmates would be remarkable because they would become more aware of the realities of the world around them. Life would become more intense in that they would begin to actually experience it for the first time."—James George

"I left a lot of baggage in the gym."—Rick Smith

I received a call from Ron Cavanaugh in late 2005 and learned that the Vipassana program was being invited to return to Donaldson. I was delighted. With a new commissioner at the Alabama Department of Corrections and a new warden at Donaldson, Ron felt that the coast was cleared of the old opposition. Bruce and Jonathan were ready to offer a three-day refresher course for the Dhamma Brothers in January, with the hope that there would be another ten-day course which would include new students in the not-too-distant future.

John Johnson
January 2006

Dear Bruce,

Greetings from Alabama. A few weeks ago I was asked if I would be willing to take part in a three-day Vipassana course in the Gym—I was momentarily suspended in time. Then thoughts came rushing into my head. At first I wondered if someone was "being cruel" with a poor sense of humor—then I realized that Ms. Brickie would not allow such a ludicrous question unless it was correct.

Oh boy, am I happy. I wanted to offer over one thousand bows of gratitude to her and the whole universe that is in alignment for "Vipassana" at Donaldson—again.

Enclosed is a news clipping that appeared in the Birmingham News a couple of months ago. You will see how "Vipassana" is greatly needed in Alabama prisons—to help the prisoners find a way out of suffering, the misery of their ignorance, to the actual cause of addiction, their harmful living. For the past ten months that I have been living in this treatment program I have come to understand much more about the "Nature of substance abuse." I see how prisoners who "realized Dhamma" with Vipassana would have access to a way out of their harmful living.

For me, the skills that Vipassana brought to me have helped me to live life as a willing human being instead of an angry person because the script of what happens was not what I wanted to happen. This actually empowered me to be happy even when things are difficult. Seeing Dhamma with insight continues to amaze me.

It is very interesting that around the week I learned about Vipassana coming to Donaldson again I was wondering how I could do another four-day course on my own as I did last year at this time.

In an effort to make a wise choice of how I prepare for this January course, I am doing Anapana-sati "for the right concentration" so that I will have used the "pre-course days with insight."

Sending Metta and Peace to the universe.

John

Interview with Wayne Finch

Jenny: **It's been four years. How are you feeling now about the return of Vipassana?**

I feel great about it, you know, and I feel that it needs to come back due to everything that's going on. They tried to stop it as a group meditation, and I feel that it's something that needs to be done. In a group you get more out of it.

You get more out of it in a group?

In a group more than just single. Because you're meditating and you feel a lot more. I feel a lot more comfortable meditating with a group, because I feel that each individual puts off this vibe that just come off the next person. And it's just an energizer knowing that you are with ten or 20 more. They're doing the same thing but dealing with different emotions and feelings.

Have you been meditating yourself over the past four years?

Yes, on and off. It hasn't been a steady everyday thing, but I meditate on weekends sometimes. Sometimes at night I might get me an hour of meditation, but it's not an everyday thing. You know, it's hard to meditate being in a closed down environment with three folks because of [people going] in and out. It will mess up your concentration.

How did you make the decision to attend the first course four years ago?

Well, the way I made a decision, Doctor Marshall came to me about it and at first I was skeptical about coming, all the way up until the day that we supposed to came in, like today. Well, really what motivated me to go into the course was OB and Kennedy. Because I really didn't want to go in at the last minute. It was like thirty minutes before we had to come in and I was like, no, I ain't going to go, man. I can't take not talking and not being able to smoke. I said I don't believe I'm going to go. Then one of them talked to me and asked me, come on and go. You know you're going to enjoy it. You know I feel that we all need it. So, they talked me into coming. And once I got in, first four days it was like, I ain't liking it, I ain't feeling it. Then about my sixth day I was ready to quit. I was actually ready to walk out. They say we can leave when we get ready, so I was telling them I was ready to go. I went and talked to Jonathan and Rick, and they talked to me and encouraged me to stay on in the course. You know, said that it will be a help, will get better by the eighth or ninth day. And I went ahead and stayed. And about the seventh day I was really getting the feeling of working with my sensations and my emotions, and I'm feeling things. And it's just, it was amazing. At the last minute, all that I been suppressing and trying to dodge start coming up. And I started dealing with a lot of emotions to the point to where I had to take a break from it. I had to come up out of my meditation stage to keep from, I guess I call it, going over the edge. And after the tenth day, it was like 'poof.' It was, like, just beautiful. I just really enjoyed it, you know. And it stayed with me after that and I continued to work with my meditation because we were working as a group once we came out. We was meeting like every other day. We was going for an hour here, come back that evening, do another hour. And the silence was good because it was a group and it felt, I believe, all of us was more comfortable being together meditating than just being a single meditating.

And then eventually you weren't able to meet anymore, right?

No, we weren't able to meet anymore, so we had to meditate on our own. And that's whenever time allowed you to meditate, in the blocks or in the dorms. We had to just take it upon ourselves to do it.

And how did you feel about that?

I felt bad about it to the point to where I even went and talked to Dr. Marshall about it, to figure out why we can't meditate, what's the reason for it. And we just got that they don't want us meditating as a group, but we can meditate single, you know. And I feel like meditating as a group is more unity, and I feel like everyone will be more in tune with each other and able to communicate a lot more better, being in the environment that we in.

So what was it like for you yesterday, seeing Bruce and Jonathan?

It felt good. It was beautiful because for me I ain't seen them in four years. And we know that it's going to be all right. That unity is back together. And to see them still working hard to try to continue to give instructions, you know, is something that we need. And concerning the emotions, they there. And they be with you on a daily basis even when you walk in, after you finish meditating, something that just stick with you. And you can feel it.

How did you prepare yourself to come here?

We came in this morning about seven to bring our mattress and bags to leave them. So when I left and went back to the block, I was more ready to get away from being around everybody, to shut down for us not talking, so I could prepare myself to come here for the three-day treatment. To where I just go ahead and go and get into my meditation. That way it will be easier for me once I get here, to the point where I won't be communicating verbally, you know. And I'm ready for the three days. I'm ready to go through them and do them.

Was that different from the first course?

Well, when I first came in to the ten-day course I had a lot more negativism about myself that I didn't have when I come out of the ten-day course! Because basically that's what I was really working on through my meditation, all that was coming up, the negativism and the anger that was within me. And I was able to deal with it through my meditation of ten days, and it helped to make me be more aware of those emotions even when I'm not meditating. So I'm able to better deal with them, you know, just walking around and being around other folks. I can deal with them better now due to my meditation stages. You know, it's a help to the point to where I don't react to a lot of things that I used to react to. I'm more aware of it. I see it, and I deal with it in a different manner now than I used to. So it has helped me make a big difference in my life. And hopefully these three days will make an even bigger difference.

One last thing. I remember you were telling me to say "Hi" to Edward.

Edward Johnson, yes.

And about how you saw a big change after the course?

Yeah, with Edward Johnson, he changed a lot because he was just coming out of lockup, did two years in lockup. I think it was like two or three weeks after he was out they had the ten-day course coming up, and he was able to get in at the last moment. And I was more looking at like, oh man, he ain't going to make it, you know, because we go way back. We been doing time together awhile, man. And I was, like, he ain't going to make it. And I was even thinking, I ain't going to make it, you know. But both of us, we pull it through and he dug down and dealt with a lot of things that he had been going through. And once them ten days was over with, the last day, I can see the big difference in him. You know, it's just like, you just see the glow on his face, the difference that it made with him to a point to where he started seeing things in a different manner. And it was a big help to him, and I was glad to see him make it through it because we had always said, "20 in, 20 out." That's the way we came in, "20 in and 20 out." So we dealt with a lot of emotions that needed to be dealt with, and I was glad to see that we was able to do that. I just wish him the best too. I just hate that he's not here to go through this three-day course with us.

Rick Smith
January 14, 2006

Dear Jenny,

It is Saturday and it is a remarkable day . . . 25 years ago on this day I was arrested and locked up. Today was a wonderful day. I want to formally thank you, Dhamma Sister, and express my gratitude to you for sponsoring the wonder-filled event! It was truly great to see you again and the experience of this course will last a lifetime.

Bruce, Jonathan and Daniel [volunteer server] were wonderful. Leon worked extremely hard. He and I are neighbors. We

sleep head to head. Our heads aren't three feet apart when we
sleep. What happened for me this course was amazing. I was in
"need." I needed an answer to my suffering! I found the answer.
I made a vow to myself that I would practice the Vipassana
technique and no other from now on and trust the purity of the
Buddha's teaching. My goal is simple, to enjoy an equanimous
mind so that I can experience liberation from the past. I will
sit one hour two times a day, morning and evening. I will let
the light of the Vipassana shine in my life and not worry about
tomorrow or anything else. I will surrender to the Dhamma. A
simple path...breath and sensation. I will keep it light. I left a
lot of baggage in the Gym. I told Bruce I would honor Dhamma
in all my affairs.

Please give Bruce, Jonathan and Daniel, along with the
people who prepared our food and served us in any capacity,
the "hope" of Dhamma from all of us who would have went for
the three-day course even if the food was regular prison food.
We appreciate the dana of one and all.

I feel with all my heart that the truth of Dhamma will shine
in the individual practice of each of the true Dhamma warriors
here. I needed this course with all of my being. I have been
experiencing Depression for months and it was making me
sick. I saw it clearly on the second day and by day three I was
certain of my answer and was ready to commit to it. I need to
be related to Universal Law.

I have thought of you often in the metta sessions at the
closure of my sittings. I am so proud of you for your work and
effort with us. I pray the determination you have shown with
the film will help so many that it cannot be counted or imagined.

I can hear Mr. Goenka's voice speaking as clear as a bell in
my mind/spirit. Be happy, peaceful . . . liberated!

Much Metta, *Rick*

Torrence Barton
January 17, 2006

What's up Jonathan,

I'm busy trying to maintain my sanity in this asylum. You're
lucky. You were fortunate enough to only encounter those of
us who still have enough screws in place to keep us mentally
stable. Even in saying that, those screws need tightening at
times, as in the meditation practice for example. That's the
very reason some of us would feel blessed to partake in the
experience on a more consistent basis. That's why I stressed the
significance of you all arriving when you did. Don't assume it
was just the practice. The compassion and understanding that
flowed from the vibe I detected was both touching and inspiring. Being instructed to use the method of Anapana at times
when my focus strays from its objective or when dealing with
life's issues prevents me from becoming overwhelmed by the
obstacles placed in my path and keeping me from becoming
stagnant as the result of it as I strive for growth and development. Sometimes I wonder why fate led me to stumble across
the precious gems of knowledge, wisdom and understanding
behind these tormenting walls. I would've been just as content
having obtained the three under normal conditions. Do you
believe in the saying, "Everything happens for a reason?"

As I said I would, I've enclosed a brief poem I wrote. It
reflects my feeling on the meditation experience:

Guiding Light

The gleam in my eyes reflects the flame igniting my spirit,
resembling that of a candlelight which burns internal discontentment.
Aware that my being should be glowing as bright as the sun shines,
thus I am driven.

Wakefulness, discipline and peace are my destination.
Carpooling with others ensures me of my arrival.
The brilliance of their rays confirms for me, "They know the way."

Peace be unto you,
Torrence Barton

John W. Johnson
January 29, 2006

Dear Jenny,
Greetings!

Now to the January 2006 three-day course. That was <u>the</u> <u>most</u> difficult course yet. Also, I realize that this was the most direct Vipassana course that I have experienced. It is very clear that the course has given me the "strength and discipline" to do a much more skilled daily practice than I imagined I would have at this stage of this practice. I am very ready and willing to do serious practice and service for another ten day course at Donaldson prison with fifty students. I see how this could be done and have spoken with prisoners who are voicing a willingness to learn this precious but serious practice of the way out of misery.

It is true. They are watching us, I will continue to practice as a noble student so that I will offer the "Courage to be at peace" even while doing time—facing truth of reality— Dhamma—changing, constantly changing.

Been reading a profound book, "A Manual of the Excellent Man" by Venerable Ledi Sayadaw, free-flow of Dhamma teachings. By far the most illuminating exploration of the "five aggregates" I have come to understand and ponder in my practice so far.

A point of interest at the three-day course was a storm I went through on "day one"—as I worked so hard and serious. Thoughts kept arising about the past few days— the contact of so much compassion—prisoners working so hard to put together the structure for a course—their questions and curious nature—the energy contact—the problems being resolved with determination—the willingness of administration—then contact with outside Dhamma Brothers and Sisters—looking into the eyes of the phenomenon that is called "collective consciousness"—pondering the impact that the effort of the past had brought into the present—gratitude beyond understanding—reflection of the self course—sadness of the suffering at Donaldson—sadness and grief for the ignorance of those who are blind to Dhamma—pain in my back, pain in my legs—agitated at not being able to remain awake with Anapana—wondering if I really wanted to be meditating anymore.

Day two—pleased day one was gone—ready for Vipassana practice to start—pondering [whether] I really wanted to be sitting—Anapana moments were lasting longer—thoughts arising about the tidal wave of last year—realizing the power of nature is beyond the control of civilization —realizing no safety with nature—amazed at the use of Pali for each student to repeat for the teaching request to learn Vipassana—more sorrow for the people of the world who suffer the impact of nature—then a free flow of tears from my eyes—it seemed to be a tidal wave of tears—it was then that the hindrances flowed away and then came Samadhi with strength—it was then I practiced with confidence with sympathetic joy & happiness that I was at the right place with the right practice at the right moment.

After that, the realization of Dukkha (suffering)—Anicca (impermanence) —Anatta (egolessness)—came and went as aggregates. I knew that it was now the serious work of Vipassana that I would get stronger with direct knowledge of equanimity—arising & passing away—that this was why I had come to be a student of this three day Vipassana course. Each night the discourses seemed to give exceptional and special insights on this remarkable course. That is such a gift to be offered to us at Donaldson, a priceless gift.

Jenny, I could go on and on and on.

I am going to try to work on some creative ways we might be able to come up with some more cushions for the ten-day course. We will need some. Can't enable future students to seek chairs because of a shortage of floor cushions. I see that as a future concern. Vipassana is a practice to be learned sitting on the ground.

Huge amounts of Metta from Donaldson,

John

James George
February 6, 2006

Dear Jenny,

Well, today marks three weeks since the completion of our three-day course and I have pretty much wound down. I suffered a great deal of physical pain during this course and I was really concerned about this. It was only after learning that I had an inflamed nerve in my lower back that I finally felt relief. A week of taking anti-inflammatory medication and I was fine.

Unfortunately I was unable to focus like I wanted and therefore feel I cheated myself. I had been truly anticipating this opportunity to work more deeply than I am able with my daily practice and at first I was very disappointed. However, once the pain was gone and I began thinking rationally, I realized what happened was exactly as it should have been, and I grew from the experience.

From what Bruce told us there are plans to hold a third ten-day course here in May; and I pray it reaches fruition. Jenny, I know Vipassana can make a significant impact on the system if only it is embraced. The change in the thinking of the inmates would be remarkable because they would become more aware of the realities of the world around them. Life would become more intense in that they would begin to actually experience it for the first time.

I know when I became aware, it was as though an entire world opened up to me. I began to love life, and when you truly love life you must love every living thing, thus you love every human being. What a concept! If I love my fellow man, how could I possibly wish him harm or cause him pain.

Jenny, I am so grateful that four years ago I was blessed with the opportunity to experience Vipassana, and I truly love all of you involved in bringing it to Donaldson.

I'll be looking forward to seeing you in May.

Much Metta,
James

Willie Carroll
February 10, 2006

Supreme Greetings Jenny!

Jenny, I had written a letter days after returning from our
last three-day sitting in the gym. To tell you a little about how
things went for me—inside and outside overall. As you remember I sat through ten days back in 2002. Well believe it or not,
these three [days] were the hardest. Jonathan and Rick had me
assigned to a corner in the gym along side the wall. Everything
I learned in the first sitting was there for me, however, the lack
of continuing sitting—although on a [now] and then basis—
wasn't enough to ward off the demons I fought on that mat.

As you know I'm in a twelve-step program here; have five
and a half years of after-care working the steps daily. However,
working the fourth step was half-ass done by me when I should
have been completely honest.

When we first entered Monday, I knew before I sat the
first hour I'd not done my homework correctly! On day two,
I (in my corner) got a chance to come all the way clean with
myself. No matter how much we (I) pray, there's always that
something I've done wrong to someone, something, somehow.
And regardless of how petty I think it was—the hurt was bigger
and needed fixing. Jenny, a lot of stuff attacked me on day
three—I felt I was being picked on, my mind focused on the
people around me until there was nobody left but me! On that
day I found if not peace but an understanding about myself. I
give thanks to all the staff members involved in making those
three days possible. The pain in a lot of ways helped to heal old
hurts within me that I had tried to just not face . . . Vipassana
really is something very special. I did have fears about my lack
of daily sittings before doing the [course] closing. Lesson well
learned! Now, daily, I do morning sitting for sixty minutes—
five to six a.m., before I start my day. Here in prison such a
sitting to meditate offers a peace of mind in a really dangerous
environment. Now I'm able to sit and seriously seek guidance,

a better state of mind before facing people around me, my day goes better. Not that I feel saved or happy—I do feel secure in how I'll react or act today . . . I've spoken to others that do as I'm doing—they too tell a story of being able to handle their days better after sitting early in the morning . . .

Jenny, being a prisoner ain't easy especially if you've lived here 26 straight years and have experienced a hard-core prisoner life, then strive to change what you've come to enjoy—no matter how wrong it was. That's in a nutshell—me. However, the road to recovery twelve step program has given me a new life. Vipassana offered further more great freedom where none was. So now, I'm okay Jenny with who I am—I do not dig where I'm at, but its okay. Things will change for the better one day. Until then, I'll continue doing what I can to better myself and offer the best I can to my brothers and to life itself.

You're always in my prayers;
Willie Carroll

February – November 2006
Appreciation to the Wardens; Dhamma Rolls On

"If we could get a permanent curriculum established [at Donaldson or St. Clair], it would be fully beneficial to all the Dhamma family and to the prisons themselves."—OB Oryang

"To be grounded in reality there has to be some sort of source. Vipassana puts me in touch with what is, the appearances of people, events and this place called prison. I no longer get thrown off center by the distractions."—Rick Smith

"Vipassana produces an objective mind… All my life, I've heard old adages that resemble 'you must love yourself.' Vipassana allows me to love myself and then I can care for others from the core of that love…."—Rick Smith

"Between breathing and the observation of it and the awareness of sensations you can take inventory of your state of mind at any time. It's a practical way to reality."—Rick Smith

"Whether you are in prison or in the free world there is no difference in the "mind." The names are just names, just symbols laying on top of sensations . . . . energy and matter."—Rick Smith

John Johnson
February 4, 2006

Attn: Warden Jones and Deputy Warden Hetzel
Donaldson Correctional Facility
Re: Vipassana Meditation Course

Dear Sirs:

Thank you for your time. This letter will be brief and to the point. For the purpose of clarity since you have two inmates with the name John Johnson, I am the one with the facial birthmark. In addition, I am 55 years of age with over 25 years of prison incarceration; Florida Department of Corrections 1977-1983; Alabama Department of Corrections 1985-1988; and 1989 to present.

Warden Jones, with all of these years of "doing time" (prison or street time), never have I witnessed a "Detoxification Process" so powerful, so real, as what I have experienced with these Vipassana courses. As a correctional official, you may have heard prisoners talk about the "reality check" that is experienced when getting busted . . . that is a powerful moment, I have to admit—although the difference is that when most criminals are caught and busted—denial is [still] found in criminal thinking activity. There is no clear moment of clarity because of denial attachments.

Now in a Vipassana course, you come "face to face" with another encounter with the police—the "process of self-policing"—and enter into a realization of your own psycho-physical realm. That ain't easy either, being "face to face" with your own reality!!! Each student must face their own mental formations and start realizing the attachments that brought them suffering with painful entanglements. But as you continue to practice Vipassana Meditation with serious effort, these barriers start to dissolve. There is then a radiant sense of happiness with a freedom from the addictive attachments that brought suffering; then comes courage to be at peace with the truth as your reality and with the sincere wish for happiness and well-being of others. This I have experienced and have heard other students admit this similar phenomenon.

Of course, the inconstant nature of the mind, mixed with the power of perception-delusions are always near and waiting to taint our inner peace. This is where the strength of practice brings wisdom so that these storms in life can be weathered out. For me, I have found that the atmosphere of living in a structured environment like the S.A.P. [Substance Abuse Program] is helpful. I too have seen the importance to maintain the discipline with two one-hour Vipassana meditations daily (morning/evening).

In closing, if you have any questions about the importance of future Vipassana Courses at Donaldson, please ask. I offer great appreciation to you and all the staff that were willing to allow Donaldson inmates to learn a practice that opens a path for harmony with reality.

I wish you all well being.

Sincerely yours,
John W. Johnson

cc:
Dr. Ron Cavanaugh, Director of Programs,
  Alabama Dept. of Corrections
Bruce Stewart, Vipassana Meditation Teacher
Denise Brickie, Substance Abuse Program Counselor,
  William E. Donaldson Prison

Benjamin Oryang
May 4, 2006

Dear Jenny,

On this end we are continuing to survive. In early March,
we (John, Omar, Milton, Johnny Mack, Rick Smith and I)
started meeting every Saturday morning for group sittings.
Dr. Marshall (who no longer works here as of May 2) availed
us with the tools and use of the group room and, even though
the meetings are not official, our consistency had made it seem
so. No announcement is made or weekly permission needed,
as we all just make our own way to the group room at about 7:
30 a.m. The officers are used to us and wave us out of our units
with terms like "Oh, you going to that meditation thing?" Of
course I have to get there before the others to get the room
open and from time to time still have to go check on one or
the other of our Dhamma brothers, but we have pretty much
established ourselves. Along with the "official" Wednesday
meetings we now have two opportunities for group sittings. I
don't know how well things will go now that Dr. Marshall is no
longer here to back us up and we have no idea what the next
psychologist will be like or if they will even allow us to use the
facilities, but we are just going to continue doing the same
thing until we are stopped or thrown out. I must mention that
Finch and Singletary also show up from time to time and there
are quite a few other people looking forward to an opportunity
to sit their first ten-day course.

I have not wavered with my daily sittings. Several guys
in my unit, including my cell-mate, question me daily about
the practice and about what they can do to help speed up the
process so that they too can learn the technique.

I think the atmosphere at St. Clair [Correctional Facility] is
more conducive than the one at Donaldson for the establishment of a more permanent Vipassana curriculum. At the same
time I know that if we could get a permanent curriculum
established at either of the prisons, it would be fully beneficial

to all the Dhamma family and to the prisons themselves. Please tell me what you think about this.

Tons of metta,

OB

Willie Carroll
May 6, 2006

Supreme Greetings, Jenny!

I'm still in the Road to Recovery program working daily under Ms. Johnson and the others. Trying to continue accepting simple instructions on how to live life on life terms—clean of drugs and criminal behavior. So far, I am doing fine, enjoying it too. Yes I do sit quietly in the mornings for thirty to forty-five minutes—and at night I do basically the same before going to sleep. So far there's no group sittings—I'm cool doing my own thing. It works. My work in the program offers me lots of chances to see just how much I've learned and gained from the sitting. There's so much stuff still within me that I have to deal with constantly in order to keep peace toward others around me—that I know meditation sincerely helps. Even under pressure from other inmates that I know in my past—I'd have done more harm than good—I now can humbly wait them out and literally meaningfully say I'm sorry for a wrong—or continue to share advice to help solve one . . . I'm a mountain away from the sun, but closer than yesterday!

That's my own motto for continuing living better than I have been. Well, Jenny, that's really all that's been going on with me. Until then, keep the prayers alive and I'll do the same.

A friend,

Willie Carroll

Rick Smith
June 26, 2006

Dear Jenny,

Greetings and Namaste! Ms Johnson talked to me today and told me about the "book." Sounds like a great idea. I also told Grady.

In this letter I'm going to talk a lot about meditation and what happens for me personally with Vipassana. The practice of Vipassana twice a day is an incredible commitment to say the least. It reduces life to this "microcosm" in relationship with all things in all ways. Each day in this prison, life presents situations that are out of prisoners' control and it challenges commitment and the confrontations we all have in place.

Unlike people who practice in the free world who can predict their time to sit for an hour and not experience interference. Also the place in which you get to sit. In prison we are like nomads, I sit in several places according to what day it is and is it morning or night. You can be right in the middle of a practice and the guards scream "count time" and sensation jumps all over you and you learn to walk Vipassana to your line and then return to the practice without internal disturbance throwing you off. You observe the sensations which can become quite gross in such an abrupt halt. You begin to experience it as the actual pattern of life itself . . . .reality! All day long each and every day, we fade in and out of comfort zones of predictability. Vipassana in its ancient principle allows me to stay in touch with the here and now. To be grounded in reality there has to be some sort of source. Vipassana puts me in touch with "what is." The appearances of people, events and this place called prison. I no longer get thrown off center by the distractions.

Vipassana produces an objective mind. Not so much in the beginning. The continual practice day in and day out introduces you to a different kind of relationship—a relationship with yourself. All my life, I've heard old adages that resemble "you must love yourself." Vipassana allows me to love myself and then I can care for others from the core of that love—at the end of practice you are ready to send metta to the universe and its inhabitants.

In this past month my life has had serious issues arise. My wife has serious medical health problems, my legal journey through the state court system has been extremely stressful and with severe roller coaster ups and downs emotionally. I've had several health issues myself. I've had some difficult classes and students. The practice of Vipassana has kept me centered during it all. Between breathing and the observation of it and the awareness of sensations you can take inventory of your state of mind at any time. It's a practical way to reality.

Oh there will be "storms." I experience days-- I used to think those storms only happened during the ten-day retreat "Vipassana course"—I was wrong. . . .The day to day practice without using other techniques along the way keeps the purity alive and the wisdom fresh . . .

Whether you are in prison or in the free world there is no difference in the "mind." The names are just names, just symbols laying on top of sensations . . . energy and matter.

Passive awareness . . . .

Well, Jenny I will close for now and do some reading and study for my new lesson plans for the classes. Blessings.

Much Metta,
Rick

Rick Smith
July 26, 2006

Dear Jonathan,

I could appreciate what you had to say about how one feels after they sit a course and the way it affects the mind.

I think/feel/perceive/intuit/experience Vipassana as a less complicated, more practical way of staying in touch with the here and now. Vipassana does away with the intellectual and leaves thought alone. With the focus on breath and sensation one doesn't get caught up in the gimmicks of therapies. The passive awareness of an objective mind is critical to the here and now. By sitting daily morning and night the mind becomes purer by nature and "who I am" appears. Down deep all of us are kind, loving people who have a lot to give. Life has so much negativity in it, not in and of itself, but it's the energies we are exposed to.

Most therapies are like religions in the methodology. Because of all the "stuff" we have pushed down and down into our subconscious minds, we end up feeling like we are in a nightmare of which there is no awakening. Therapy and religions give people tools to do change in the dreams-cape and alter the nightmare into a happier dream. It's like software that goes with a computer—instead of Microsoft, it's Dreamsoft—and has windows as well. Windows within windows. Of all the dream scenarios that one can conceive just like a computer game, all the moves are in the program chip. So in the end, we go through one dream after another and we think we are awake. We are just trading dreams, we change the names, but the dynamics stay the same—mere role playing on a healthier level. There are rewards to better dreams and roles. But one is still co-dependent. You have the craving, the aversion, the lack of genuine awareness. A million ways to play it all out—one might say a lifetime. One can dream or be awake . . . the Buddha recognized the endless cycle and how desire played into it. Vipassana goes back to a science of mind where thought and the thinker become one—subject/object ceases. Vipassana leaves the practitioner witness to the movement of life and doesn't attempt to make life anything other than "what is."

What is just is; it doesn't care one way or the other. There's no comparison in it. It just is. No need to "compete," bargain, coerce oneself in any way. One sensation is no different from the other—only in our mind. As the mind becomes still, it is creative. It flows . . . the purer the mind the lack of possessing.

In silence, the mind naturally turns within to observe its own nature. We fear silence. Seeing this is the beginning of freedom. Liberation to self-examine.

To understand Vipassana, we have to go back to "intent"— why am I practicing Vipassana? Is it a doing? Or is it a be-ing? To purify the mind is a "cleansing"—I don't really have to go anywhere.

Vipassana doesn't teach me what the Universe is; it shows me "how" it works. Just being with the breath/sensation I am connected. Not to a philosophy, an idea, a concept, a tool. I am related to life right here, right now. Vipassana keeps me from the rational mind—I don't need to think about what I'm doing. The "monkey mind" will chatter . . . that's its nature. Below that is a deeper mind, the mind is like an ocean. On the surface, a lot of activity—the deeper you go toward the ocean's floor—the deeper the movement. When oxygen comes from the floor of the ocean you can't see it—it is so compressed; as it arrives at the surface all that changes.

Sankharas (conditioned mental reactions) go down into our mind and become hidden to us but have direct effects on our lives. We are a microcosm of the universe "literally."

Vipassana allows me to observe that I am attached to individual objects, property and people and [therefore] cannot experience the oneness of metta. The universal love of creation.

In the end, Vipassana can only be experienced. We can't experience it vicariously through another. We have to be it ourselves!

Before Vipassana, the closest I came to purifying the mind was with the practice of Tai Chi and the Tao philosophy by Lao-Tzu, which also goes back to the time of the birth of Vipassana through the Buddha.

Sitting in Vipassana practice is deeper because of the lack of physical movement. I experience harmony through Tai Chi and the Tao, but not "liberation." Vipassana takes all the toys away from the mind and leaves us with observing "energy"—what is energy before we name it? Where does it go? How does it change?

The observation of sensation—a God insight—the missing link—the place where all other techniques drop the ball. What causes a sensation? To track the craving/aversion cycle.

The daily practice of a pure technique like Vipassana brings clarity to life's little/big problems and you realize, "there are no problems apart from the mind" like J. Krishnamurthi once said. We are making all of it up.

Vipassana gives me peace. Life is hilarious! The freedom to laugh at my own pettiness and peculiar habits and idiosyncrasies and not take everything so personal. What a boon!

In my job description, my personal daily practice of Vipassana gives me consistency and endurance and stamina toward all the people and events that could be overwhelming if not seen objectively. It gives me practice with my students, friends and family and peers all day long every day. I need that. It helps!

Well, Jonathan, thanks for the words of encouragement and for the contribution of you toward my practice of Vipassana.

Rick

Rick Smith
August 9, 2006 *(continued)*

Dear Jonathan,

In my last letter I shared the gains from Vipassana but I left out something. Nothing I have experienced in the Vipassana practice needs more mention than the basic contact with "gratitude" I discovered so unconsciously that you almost overlook it. The silent joy you experience being connected to the source [when you meditate] two times a day. No matter what arises, the being grounded in the silent joy of absolute gratitude is a "safe-haven" for mankind. I can't fix all this stuff (out there). However, I can observe my body's reaction to it through sensation. I can passively become aware of the craving for moreness, the accumulation of stuff and/or the aversion to stuff I've named bad/negative/not comfortable etc., etc. I do not have to have any social status whatsoever to be rich, wealthy, and empowered through the objective awareness of the mind. Peace. It was in the last place I thought to look. Imagine that? Exactly, imagination has a tendency to move one away from peace. What happens when we stop doing? What is left?

No peace without gratitude. Tears flow down your face and you don't "know" why or even care. It just happens. It's beautiful to live, to love (metta), to experience silent joy. What a gift. The gift of the highest to the highest. A process absent of subject/object. It's why we can't explain Vipassana. Only practice introduces the truth. The purity. The real essence. My oasis.

Blessing and metta to you and our Dhamma family! Thanks for your selflessness in all you are, my brother. Much metta to you!!!

Peace, Namaste,
Rick

John Johnson
July 2006

Dear Jenny,

The hot dog days of southern summer are here upon us again. Over the years of doing time in the South I have dreaded summer. But even that seems to have changed. Is it because in my elder years I am more tolerant? Or is this another sign of freeing the attachments from even environmental discomforts that the Vipassana technique has helped me with?

Doing time is never comfortable. There are always feelings of inadequacy that arise and can be very discouraging—even after a one-hour deep Vipassana meditation.

I remember recently walking onto the exercise yard to watch a sunset—this was a very aesthetic pleasure moment too—I was listening to my radio, "Echos" on National Public station—my kind of music—subtle sensations flowing all around—feeling free in moments of watching sky flowing too—you know what I mean—being one with Nature . . .

Then here came another person who looked up at the sky with me. I said, "Hello . . . isn't this sunset powerful?"

He said, "Yeah"—but I sensed that he felt distressed—I said the usual ice breaker, "What's up?"

He said, "I think I'm going to kill myself."

I thought, "Man, you just blew my communing with the sky—how can you not feel this energy?" I did not like the discourse I was facing. Although I did know the history of this person: he had messed his life up years ago killing another convict. I could not take lightly that he could maybe be serious about taking his own life. I would now listen with a compassionate ear and send metta [generate loving-kindness] to him.

After a few moments of talking, up came another convict—still an awe inspiring sunset in the sky—this guy says, "I'm really pissed off at so-n-so, I am tired of his shit, I think I am going to stab his ass and let him know who I am!"

I think, "why is this happening to me?—I just want to be happy and watch this sunset . . ."

But I too know the history of this guy. He has been in prison for over 20 years and has committed murder too. I must share metta with him and listen with a compassionate ear with him also.

After a few moments, the guy who wanted to kill himself said, [to the other convict] "I can't believe that after all the time you have done, you would let someone get you going like that. Just let it go!"

How about that!! Now the person who wanted to end his own life is helping to save the life of two other people. An unexpected twist. Very powerful experience, Jenny. Dhamma phenomena that I never would have dreamed I would have experienced going to watch the sunset on Donaldson's prison yard. Now with a few months of time passed these guys are reacting to a better outlook of doing time. Did my metta make any difference? Who knows? I do know that the metta helped me through that experience of all of us, suffering and seeing misery. Years ago I would not have had this metta experience as a tool in facing the reality of doing time.

In retrospect, I see how my quality of doing time with a non pardonable sentence started changing. I started seeing another way of seeing the world while taking the Houses of Healing course. Like an awakening process unfolding. It was there where I had the realization that the endless stream of thoughts and feelings that ran through my mind . . . were only a flux of the damaged inner child. This helped me to see why my self-centered desires, needs, expectations, were the fears that I projected falsely in my view of the world or life according to my damaged inner child that was satisfied and happy when things went my way and upset if they did not.

Now when these negative traits with underlying feelings of the damaged inner child come up—I see the whole picture show. Robin's teachings also showed me that I had the inner power to "stop the show here." Where I am—still doing time—still with life without parole—still not always getting my way—even while caught in between powerful dhammas like at the prison yard sunset experience.

Everything since the Houses of Healing course has seemed to open a kindred relationship to life. When Vipassana came to Donaldson, it was as if it was just natural that I was learning such a lineage of meditation. This was just what was supposed to happen. All the free-world Vipassana people seemed kindred. The Four Noble Truths were a natural truth. Dhamma recognition became known. The teachers were serious teachers of Dhamma that is still beyond my words to express. In my whole life experience suta-maya-pañña (wisdom gained by listening to others) along with cinta-maya-pañña (intellectual, analytical understanding) has been a part of the aggregates that I have dealt with not realizing what was beyond it all. Until bhavana-maya-pañña (wisdom based on direct personal experience) came to Donaldson.

In that direct personal experience, I found five friends [faith, effort, awareness, concentration and wisdom] that would be strengths to withstand the storms of life. The five hindrances [craving, aversion, agitation, sloth, doubt] still come flowing at me. Each one of them attack me. As I know attack you and everyone else. Watch the news on TV; look at the faces of people in the world.

I will continue with strong determination to practice Vipassana with the insight of the noble path that these compassionate Dhamma brothers and sisters brought from ages ago and distant lands to the prison in Alabama. Who would have thought that AL-A-BA-MA prisoners would be the first prison in the United States to hold a Vipassana course? I never would have thought it was possible. This shows how powerful kamma [karma] is. Vipassana in prisons is of great importance. Recognize this reality that is happening right now at this maximum prison in Alabama. With your reading of this report you are a part of this kamma. Thank you for your efforts and generosity to bring these precious teachings into Donaldson. Thank you for your metta. May we all become stronger in cultivation of the four qualities of a pure mind. May we always practice sila (moral actions). . . samadhi (concentration). . . pañña (wisdom). . . .

> To all y'all Bhavatu Sabba Mangalam
> (May all beings be happy!) *John*

John Johnson
(No date)

Dear Jenny,

Everything is well. My fellow convicts are caught up with "war emotions." I thought a guy was going to "stick" the person he was having a heated argument about dropping bombs on innocent children in Iraq. The guy who wanted to protect the children from violence was going to use violence to prove his "correctness" of the issue.

Nothing happened except throwing verbal darts. How easy it could have gone out of control though.

With some of my fellow convicts I just say, "I do not know."
Then I send metta.

Peace, *John*

John W. Johnson
August 29, 2006

Dear Jonathan,

Thank you for your letter. It is incredible, the size of the
pagoda construction project in Mumbai. What an extraordinary
thought that it will hold 8000 meditators and will be visible
from outer space—wow! Do you think that there will really be
8000 people to sit together? Will they all be Vipassana meditators? Eight thousand—sadhu, sadhu, sadhu! [Well said, well
said, well said!]

I honor the fact that we at Donaldson are part of shared
experiences that we transmit as we encounter life. Just as each
of y'all are [part of] shared experiences of pañña (wisdom) as
we encounter life at Donaldson Prison. This also means the
relationships we have with family and free-world friends.

This thought of everyday interactions is one that I have
found to be "precious engagement." At first, after the first ten-
day course—how to interact—was full of hindrances. Do you
get my drift? Here I am at a maximum prison sitting still twice
a day—smiling a lot, no longer eating stolen food from [the]
kitchen, quiet at times, talking at other times . . . (but, not as
argumentative as I have been in the past), agitation of doing
time not as pronounced [as witnessed] by people who knew
me and my radical nature. I quit chewing tobacco products, no
longer bored, each moment having an experience to note and
let go . . .

Some of my fellow convicts thought I had been over taken
by the "hostage syndrome." That is where a prisoner becomes
brain-washed and succumbs to being held captive, making
friends with guards and accepting incarceration.

Of course, Dhamma practice is about the way to liberation, not bondage. How does a person interact in prison? I have yet to find a "how to" book for convicts. This is where I realized that myself and my fellow Donaldson Dhamma brothers would have to be "Dhamma warriors." With the three trainings of sila (moral conduct), samadhi (concentration) pañña (wisdom), we would blaze a path! You know how that works out . . . "things happen that we do not want; things that we want do not happen."

We did have another ten-day course and I was even allowed to be a student at that course. I thought, "How wonderful, I am greatly going to improve my faculty of self-observation through another Vipassana course." Well, truth observation hit me from the "top of my head to the bottom of my toes." The course was held during a May Alabama heat spell. I was in summer heat misery. Also a prison construction project had an earth mover that made very loud crunching noises and a loud annoying bell that heavy equipment uses when backing up. When I expressed my disappointment to the teacher, he started smiling and said, "Good!" Then he explained that it would help me to go to "bodily sensations" and not grasp at "agitation and worry" with the environmental conditions.

With this being the second prison course, I had already realized anicca (impermanence), anatta (egolessness), dukkha (suffering), so I allowed the storm to pass.

Even after the second course, "every day interactions" were not as I expected them to be. It became uncertain that there would ever be another course at Donaldson. We were no longer allowed to have group sittings. No one could explain why. We just knew that this was a sankhara (conditioned mental reaction) that appeared to be arising from who knows where. Because we had a precious opportunity to acquire the tools of Dhamma and were taught about how *saddha* (faith), *viriya* (effort), *sati* (awareness), *samadhi* (concentration) and *pañña* (wisdom) would aid us during these experiences of problems with aggregates—that we with *adhitthana* (great determination) acquire *parami* (virtues that lead to Liberation). Goenkaji sat with us at Donaldson on the final day of the second course and gave instruction to work with the three trainings and that it was not going to be easy. But it was of great importance to help others at Donaldson to open a path of Dhamma at Donaldson. And in doing so, our first responsibility is to live a healthy, harmonious life, good for ourselves and for all others—because they would be watching us.

Since that last day of that second course of Vipassana at Donaldson, we Dhamma brothers who are "Dhamma Warriors" are living a "How-To Life" at Donaldson. We're spread out through this prison. Some of the interactions are made in substance abuse programs, as educational aides, as aides in the medical infirmary, helping law library research, even living in the worst of worst cell blocks as compassionate beings.

Sometimes we don't make wise choices and we experience all kinds of hindrances with the fruit of wrong action. This comes with being human. Most times a prisoner has many more sankharas (conditioned mental reactions) than the average human it surely seems. But, as the practice continues our four qualities of a pure mind—metta (loving-kindness), karuna (compassion), mudita (sympathetic joy), and upekkha (equanimity)—cultivates a stronger sangha (community of seekers).

So maybe someday a book will be written to aid prisoners for every day interactions—until then I guess we will still have "the way it is"—via our letters.

I have some questions on the *sampajaññam* [constant thorough understanding of impermanence] paper you sent. Thanks for that too!

Y'all take care now.

Sending metta,
John

November 29, 2006
Parole Denied

> When faced with the vicissitudes of life,
> One's mind remains unshaken,
> Sorrowless, stainless, secure;
> This is the greatest welfare.

> —*Gotama the Buddha, Mangala sutta*

Willie Carroll
November 29, 2006

Hello Jenny,

I got your card last night–the greetings was very inspiring.
Thank you—know that I'm okay. I wrote you last week after
I got settled back into my present situation. Not once have I
stopped meditating. By reaching within for strength to handle
my situation, this is why I'm okay. I'm not thrilled about five
more years after doing twenty-eight. I'd enjoy a life where I'm
to pay bills–be responsible–raise a family–see life bloom freely
without just dreaming it. However, I'm equipped with a spiritual aura that says–it's okay–just keep smiling because really
it's okay. Without that blessing I'd be insane doing things these
guys do thinking they're sane. If it wasn't for what I learned
at Donaldson from you guys and the Crime Bill program–so
yeah, it's okay. I've not given up on trying to get my freedom
physically. But I'm mentally okay and spiritually fit to handle
whatever goes down.

Not many people get the chance to do what you guys do
to change hard-core prisoners. Vipassana has truly put me in
contact with me as a person more than anything I have ever
done in my entire life. Even after being told I'll be here possibly
five more years, I'm okay. I took a spiritual beating that day.
My lower self was center stage. I fought a helluva fight that
day. But something happened during my battle to remain sane
to tell me that I'm much bigger than to give in to depression.

I'm okay. My higher being took over. Today I am gifted with my meditation, my friends, and a loving sister, and God's guidance. I don't desire freedom on won'ts, but on a will to help create something greater. So yes, Jenny, I'm okay, and hopefully will be even better someday.

Any sittings soon? I only get in forty-five to sixty minutes a day here. But even that is a blessing. You take care. Whatever I can do, it's a most times honor.

Take care,
Willie

CONCLUSION

After witnessing the Dhamma Brothers' dedication to their personal and spiritual growth, it is clear to me that public policies which abandon prisoners to long-term incarceration without the benefit of serious rehabilitation—basically to sit and wait for either death or release—are indefensibly wasteful and shortsighted. Certainly there are inmates who are beyond being helped by programs due to lack of motivation and depth of psychopathological damage. However, there needs to be a means of identifying those numerous prisoners who have the potential and desire to change. A blanket policy of locking up all inmates and denying them any means for significant personal transformation is currently creating a huge, separate social system of pariahs and outcasts. Without effective treatment, the successful reintegration of released inmates back into society as healthy and productive individuals becomes increasingly remote. The social consequences of simply discarding society's damaged and dangerously truant members are profound and troubling, whether they are kept in prison or let back out on the street.

Unfortunately we have all heard of high-profile cases when prisoners are released without the benefit of treatment, and then dramatically reoffend. These occurrences understandably fuel fear of crime. In the eighties and nineties politicians rushed to demonstrate their concern for public safety and many supported reactive legislation such as "three strikes" laws. Offenders sentenced under these laws received much longer prison sentences than those convicted in the past of the same crimes. The "get-tough-on-crime" movement was largely based on the extreme cases and quick-fix solutions. This in turn directly led to rapid growth in the prison industry generated by locking up many more nonviolent offenders, while crime rates overall remained relatively stable.[1] By 2007 there were over 2.2 million people incarcerated in the United States, the most in any country worldwide. Incredibly, this means that one in every 32 adult Americans is in prison or on supervised release. With only five percent of the world's population, we now house 25 percent of all prisoners.[2] This rate of incarceration represents a 400 percent increase since 1980.

In 2000, while the incarceration rate remained very high, the rate of release also began to increase. Partially in response to the massive prison overcrowding that resulted from the "three strikes" laws, about 700,000 prisoners were released from prison in 2007. That's 1900 per day across the country, and the release numbers are expected to increase annually over the years ahead.[3] It is considered likely that as many as two-thirds could be rearrested within three years. This revolving-door policy of catch, warehouse and release, without effective rehabilitation, only serves to create an extremely costly and hazardous erosion of public safety.

The solution is neither to hold people forever nor release them prematurely, but to make good decisions about sentencing and treatability, use the most effective programs available and then release those who are deemed to be rehabilitated. However, rehabilitation as a goal of imprisonment has been underfunded and weakened by the exorbitant costs of widespread prison expansion. This goal needs to be reestablished as a priority. In short, we need to start addressing the root causes of crime and recidivism rather than just treating the symptoms.

Judging from the early findings of the Vipassana prison program, it is clear that voluntary, nonsectarian spiritual training for prisoners can be enormously effective. The depth of inmates' misery and suffering throughout the length of their sentences makes them natural candidates for deep introspection. Although the lasting impact of offering this type of program in a prison environment needs to be examined further, there are already strong implications about what the best practices of twenty-first-century corrections could look like. The central questions to be explored include: why this program worked so well, why the men responded so positively

to its opportunity for social and psychological change despite the tremendously challenging personal efforts required, and why it was so important
to so many of them, even under the order to stop meditating together, to
continue to practice individually under difficult circumstances.

One reason for the program's success is that it provides an alternative
social system and thereby a different identity from that normally available
to inmates. Quite intentionally, there is a nameless, faceless anonymity
to prison life, with its labeled uniforms and numbered beds. It is a social
system largely lacking in the array of associations and identities afforded in
free society. Daily life inside is organized around social control, punishment
and the restriction of voluntary social groupings and affiliations. Vipassana,
by contrast, constructs a temporary, separate living space and provides
purposeful, therapeutic practices based on critically distinct values. Once
inside the course environment, students experience a profound shift away
from their deprived and stigmatized mass identity. Vipassana precepts and
guidelines respect the privacy and humanity of each student. The course
guides are the very model of loving mentors. In this insulated social world
within the larger prison system, all students are recognized as worthy
individuals in the present, regardless of events in the past. This experience
alone is uplifting.

Even more striking was the nurturing, protective role of the three corrections officers assigned to the program. Their strength of character and
understanding of the course enabled them to unfailingly provide support to
the students, their usual charges. Within this shielded cocoon, the spiritual
development of each man could gradually emerge as part of a communal
effort, drawing the men into a Vipassana brotherhood. The shared ordeal
of meditating together during long hours, coupled with the separation
and protection from the surrounding prison culture of forced control and
danger, heightened and strengthened this new sense of community.

The brothers had voluntarily left behind an institutional mode of social
organization to become part of this new, closely-knit community. They
lived dramatically apart from the world of anonymity and violence that lay
outside the locked door of their refuge. After the retreat ended and Bruce,
Rick and Jonathan departed, the men returned to the general prison population and continued to adhere to their new identity. The group was now

united by this intense, shared history. They began to turn to one another for support and guidance. Several men emerged as leaders of this ongoing

Vipassana community by staying in close touch with the others and encouraging everyone to attend the twice-daily group sittings which they had organized imme-diately after the first course. Some inmates went on to arrange and do their own retreats in their dorms or cells. All of this represented very considerable initiative on their part.

Warm greetings after the course ends

Prison normally either alienates inmates from one another or produces harmful gang behavior, so a wholesome solidarity was an important phe-nomenon for Donaldson. The group spirit lived on. The Dhamma Brothers reported that whenever they saw one another in the corridors or cell blocks, they felt like family and often embraced. This was highly unusual, since physical expressions of affection and intimacy are generally not welcomed by male prisoners. Yet, within the Vipassana community, these gestures of closeness and affection became acceptable. When a Vipassana student was sent to segregation after an incident, the Dhamma Brothers conveyed word that they all stood by him and looked forward to his return to their group sittings. Several who had previously participated in prison gang life now supported one another in their resolve to stay away from gang violence. It remains to be seen if the men will be able to maintain the social fabric of this Vipassana community over time. No matter how fervent their desire for it, the survival of their fledgling association will also depend upon the support of the broader Vipassana community outside, as well as the continued toleration of it by the correctional staff at hand.

The principle reason that the Vipassana program had such a profound effect on the participants was that it gave them an opportunity for signifi-cant introspection in a safe, supported environment. More common prison treatment programs are generally cognitive-behavioral, denoting the focus on reshaping and retraining of thoughts and behaviors. These target the dysfunctional attitudes, beliefs and activities which condition criminal thinking. Programs such as assertiveness training, anger management, relaxation techniques, violence prevention, and substance abuse relapse prevention are frequently included in prison curricula. Their goals are to reduce recidivism and eliminate habitual criminal conduct.

With Vipassana, the participants go through a more profound process of awareness and nonsectarian spirituality than is thought possible or appropriate for inmates. They come away from the program having learned to objectively observe within themselves and to develop compassion for themselves and others. The men are also enabled, perhaps for the first time in their lives, to look back with vivid awareness at their traumatic childhood histories, their addictions and even their crimes. From the depths of their collective desperation and misery, these inmate students sought nothing short of personal transformation. Adrift on the sea of their suffering, seated upon their cushions as if on life rafts, they rode out their storms together.

The success of this dramatic tale of human potential and transformation might also be attributed to the preexisting subculture of meditation and personal growth that had been fostered among the inmates at Donaldson, starting with the first inmate-led meditation groups six years earlier. Several hundred inmates had attended the Houses of Healing course, and there was a growing cadre of inmate teachers for it. Many individuals were already meditating on a regular basis. Many were also familiar with various experiences of their own spirituality and the notion that within everyone is a purer underlying nature, no matter what one's history may be. The realization of their fundamental humanity, despite their status as prisoners, helped them to summon the courage and willingness to look deep inside and commit to the potential for more change.

The direct experience of revealed inner realities as engendered by the Vipassana course came as an enormous relief. It allowed the Donaldson students not only to take responsibility for their offenses and the issues that led to their criminal behaviors, but also to move on with the capacity to generate genuine empathy for everyone affected, including themselves.

These stories of the Dhamma Brothers challenge narrow assumptions about the nature of prisons as places of punishment rather than rehabilitation and transformation. While fairer sentencing and reformed parole systems would contribute to overall improvement, only by fostering deep personal change in inmates can there be a way out of this stunningly broken cycle. If we are going to succeed in revolutionizing a deadened prison system currently committed only to warehousing and punishment, we need a correctional policy that recognizes the capacity for psychological healing and growth and offers significant opportunities and skills for such change.

---

[1]Daniel Macaillar, *From Classroom to Cell Blocks: How Prison Building Affects Higher Education and African American Enrollment in California.* 1996 (Center on Juvenile and Criminal Justice. 2002) http://www.cjcj.org/pubs/higher/highercal.html

[2]Ted Koppel, *Breaking Point: Quick Facts.* (Koppel on Discovery, 7 October, 2007) http://dsc.discovery.com/convergence/koppel/slideshows/prison-issues/prison-issues.html & http://dsc.discovery.com/convergence/koppel/highlights/highlights.html

[3]Celeste Fremon, *America the Jailor.* (Witness LA, 5 October, 2007) http://www.witnessla.com/prison/2007/admin/america-the-jailor/ & http://witnessla.com/category/prison-policy/

POSTSCRIPT

On a bright, cold day in January 2006, Bruce, Jonathan and I walked back into Donaldson. With suitcases clattering behind, we passed through the locked gates and barbed wire fencing into the familiar, dimly lit corridor. We had not seen the Dhamma Brothers in four years.

The shutdown of the Vipassana program had cast a pall across our hopes of providing ongoing support and encouragement to the men. Of course, we had received and answered their letters, but we had not been able to visit Donaldson. I always worried that we had started the Dhamma Brothers on this journey and then had been unable to continue with them. I felt as if I had abandoned them.

When I received Ron Cavanaugh's call inviting us to return to the prison, I was ecstatic. Ron and I had stayed in close touch over the years, and he had always maintained that we should simply wait for the right moment to return.

When we arrived the Dhamma Brothers were standing in the hallway outside the entrance to the West Gym. They stood motionless in a long line as we approached them. Prisoners are taught to remain exactly where they are told and to move only when instructed. They lose the freedom to make their own choices. The Dhamma Brothers now quietly stood their ground, but their faces told a very different story of joy and excitement. Several of them were weeping with happiness. I was overwhelmed with emotion, struggling to regain composure. We stared at one another, unclear what to do next.

Bruce broke the silence by greeting them. "Hi guys. Jonathan and I have the dubious distinction of being the only guys who ever wanted to come back to Donaldson. All you guys want out; we want to come back in." That was perfect. Everyone relaxed and laughed at the absurdity of the thought that anyone would be eager to get back into Donaldson.

In 2002 the film crew from Northern Light Productions and I had started working on a documentary about these events at Donaldson. That film footage and the many hours of audio-taped interviews were the precious artifacts we had initially collected with the hopes of telling these stories. Now the crew was allowed to return with me on this visit to do the filming required for completion. [*The Dhamma Brothers* film was finished in 2007 and won awards at two film festivals. Theatrical release of the film is scheduled in 2008.]

All of us spent the next two days inside the gymnasium with the Dhamma Brothers as preparations were made for a three-day Vipassana course. During this visit they told their stories of struggle, describing their efforts to stay connected to one another and to the practice of Vipassana. We filmed individual and group interviews and informal scenes as the men rested and prepared themselves for the meditation course. During the final moments before the course was to begin, there was a palpable air of serious reverence for the commencement of an important and longed-for event.

My last sight of the Dhamma Brothers was of them walking in silence and dignity to the edge of the meditation area, removing their shoes and then sitting on their meditation cushions. As Bruce and Jonathan began the course, I walked back out of Donaldson with the hope that this would not be my last visit.

The Vipassana program now seems to be firmly rooted at Donaldson. There is a new stirring of hope in its still, stale air. Ten-day courses were held in the West Gym in both May and October 2007, and the number of Dhamma Brothers is growing. Ron Cavanaugh hired a new psychologist, Dr. Kathy Allen, whose job includes developing and supporting an on-going Vipassana program. Several additional staff members, including Dr. Allen, have completed a ten-day course at a Vipassana center.

A medium-security facility several hours away, Hamilton Prison, has now begun a Vipassana program and has held two ten-day courses. Ron is now looking for potential sites at other Alabama prisons. In his characteristicly confident and unstoppable style, Ron's belief in the need for and feasibility of the Vipassana prison program has triumphed.

While the future holds no guarantees, the words of the Dhamma Brothers ring with the truth of their experiences and carry a quiet power and conviction that is difficult to resist. OB Oryang expressed it well during our visit in January 2006:

> "Donaldson is a crazy place. The most incorrigible in the Alabama prison system are put here, the high-risk people and the people who are unmanageable at other prisons. It's a jumble of confusion, a jumble of violence. Nobody is immune to it. The past two weeks have seen evidence of that. Two prisoners killed another prisoner last week, and there were seven stabbings. There has been much tension in the air. Nevertheless, there is still that sense of peacefulness among some of the guys here. Vipassana has helped guys to be able to see differently, to be more tolerant of one another, and to understand why others behave the way they do. Vipassana meditators as a group are more aware than any other group. I think Donaldson could gain a lot more from this course. If there were a hundred more prisoners walking around in here who had the mind and sense of my Dhamma Brothers, it would make a big difference."

ADDRESS TO INMATE STUDENTS

May 16, 2002, W.E. Donaldson Correctional Facility
Bessemer, Alabama

S.N. Goenka, principal teacher of Vipassana

I am so glad, so glad to be with you all this morning. I
was informed by your teacher that this course was very
successful because you all worked very hard. One has to
work very hard to get good results.

But this is just a beginning. It is a long path. You
have taken the first step. The longest journey starts
with the first step. You have taken the first step—the
right step, on the right path, in the right direction. Now

S.N. Goenka

you have to keep walking on the path. Whatever you
gained by these ten days of meditation is just the beginning—to convince
you that, "Yes, I am on the right path, I have taken the right step in the
right direction." Now you have to keep strengthening yourselves. Whatever
purity you have attained, that should not only be maintained, but it must
be increased, developed.

Understand, you have two great responsibilities now. One responsibility is, whatever you have learned here in ten days, you have to use it to
strengthen yourself. Because you were able to eradicate even a small
amount of negativity from your mind, a very good beginning has been
made. And now you know the technique—how to liberate yourself from
negativities, how to liberate yourself from misery. The more you practice,
the more strength you will get. This will be more fruitful for you. You all
understand that whatever you have practiced is not a rite or a ritual. It is
an exercise. You do physical exercise to keep your body healthy and strong.
Now you learn this mental exercise to keep your mind healthy, strong,
wholesome, happy. I am glad that the authorities here have allowed you
to practice every day—morning one hour, evening one hour. That will give
you strength.

And not just sitting morning and evening one hour each. You have to keep examining yourself: "Is any positive change coming in my life or not? Is this positive change increasing or not?" Given a similar situation previously, before taking Vipassana, how did you react? Do you have the same reaction now, or are you coming out of it? Not that all reaction will go away immediately—it will go away, a time will come. But at present a beginning has been made. So the first responsibility is to strengthen yourself in Dhamma, in this way of life. That is for your good, for your benefit, for your liberation from misery.

And you have another greater responsibility. You have hundreds of other prisoners in this prison. They will be watching you, wondering: "What did these people do for ten days? What have they gained?" They will be watching you very critically. If they find no change in you, they won't be inspired to spend ten days of their life when they have the opportunity. For ten days you were in this spiritual prison. Why would anybody willingly do that? But when they see a big change in your life, the glow on your face, the compassion in your eyes, the politeness in your behavior, and they see you so happy, so happy—they will get attracted. There will be a demand for more and more such courses. And all your fellow prisoners who are suffering, certainly suffering—they will want to start practicing and will start coming out of their misery.

I have worked with thousands of prisoners and I know what great suffering they experience. Due to whatever crime they have committed, small or big, they are kept away from their family. They are kept away from all the comforts of family life. That itself is a great misery.

But a bigger prison is the prison of one's behavior pattern. Deep inside, everyone is a prisoner of his unwholesome behavior patterns at the depth of the mind. Without knowing what one is doing, one continues generating some negativity or the other: "When I get out of jail, I will take revenge. I will teach a lesson to so and so. I will do this, I will do that." All kinds of anger, hatred, aversion.

By this technique one starts realizing: "What am I doing? Every time I generate negativity, look, I am the first victim of my negativity. I become so miserable, I become so miserable." No one wants to make himself miserable. Yet, out of ignorance you keep making yourself miserable, miserable.

And now you realize: "I've got a wonderful technique to come out of this misery."

Your fellow prisoners here, they are suffering from both these miseries—the misery of being kept away from their families and the misery of generating negativity in their minds.

If they are inspired, seeing you as a good example of Vipassana, a good product of Vipassana, they will voluntarily take courses. Then you will find the number of your comrades, your Dhamma brothers, is increasing; the whole atmosphere gets charged with love, compassion, goodwill, love, compassion, goodwill.

So this is the second responsibility you have: to help fellow prisoners to take advantage of this wonderful, scientific, nonsectarian technique. Nobody asked you to convert from one organized religion to another organized religion. The conversion is, rather, the conversion of the mind from bondage to liberation, from ignorance to enlightenment, from cruelty to compassion, from misery to happiness. This is required by one and all.

So have compassion towards your fellow prisoners here, let them be encouraged to pass through this process and start coming out of their misery, little by little.

Not only that, now your behavior here will be watched by so many people outside. Every government thinks that if we punish a criminal he will be all right. That is a wrong attitude. We have to help the person who made a mistake in the spur of the moment. Help him come out of negativity, come out of unwholesome action, both vocal and physical.

All the state governments of this country, all the governments of different countries, will be inspired to help prisoners. Show them that there is a way out, a practical way which gives results here and now. And such a scientific way—rational, pragmatic; no blind faith is involved. So many people around the world will be benefited.

Initially courses were given in an Indian prison. And when the result was so good, some of the jail superintendents told me: "I can't believe this person was such a hardened criminal. How has he become a saintly person? I can't believe it. But this is the fact. Such a big change has come." Such words start spreading.

Then the government in India issued a notification: Every prison must have Vipassana courses. So many people are getting benefited because of the example of the early inmate-students who worked in Vipassana. Their behavior started changing. That was a good example for others.

So this is a very big responsibility you are carrying. You are now living a better life, more peaceful, more harmonious, not only for your own good, but for the good of so many others, so many others.

I keep telling people that those who are behind walls are not the only prisoners. Everyone outside this wall is also a prisoner—a prisoner of his own unwholesome behavior patterns of the mind. People have to come out of that—come out of the prison, get liberated.

I am sure you will be the carriers of the message. You will shine brightly. People will look at you: "Look, what a big change has come, what a big change has come." That will inspire so many suffering people—behind the walls and outside the walls.

I am sure whatever benefits you have gained during these ten days, if you keep growing, growing in a Dhamma life, you will certainly start shining brightly, becoming a very good example to miserable people around the world.

May all of you keep growing in Dhamma. May all of you enjoy the best fruits of Dhamma. May all of you live a happy life, a peaceful life, a harmonious life—good for you and good for so many others.

Be happy, be happy, be happy.

MORE ABOUT VIPASSANA

The technique of Vipassana meditation is a simple, practical way to achieve real peace of mind and to lead a happy, useful life. Vipassana means "to see things as they really are" and is a logical process of mental purification through self-observation.

From time to time we all experience agitation, frustration and disharmony. When we suffer, we do not keep our misery limited to ourselves; instead, we keep distributing it to others. Certainly this is not a proper way to live. We all long to live at peace within ourselves, and with those around us. After all, human beings are social beings: we have to live and interact with others. How, then, can we live peacefully? How can we remain harmonious ourselves, and maintain peace and harmony around us?

Vipassana enables us to experience peace and harmony: it purifies the mind, freeing it from suffering and the deep-seated causes of suffering. The practice leads step-by-step to the highest spiritual goal of full liberation from all mental defilements.

Historical Background

Vipassana is one of the world's most ancient meditation techniques. It was rediscovered 2600 years ago by Gotama the Buddha, and is the essence of what he practiced and taught during his 45 years of teaching. During the Buddha's time, large numbers of people in northern India were freed from the bonds of suffering by practicing Vipassana, allowing them to attain high levels of achievement in all spheres of life. Over time, the technique spread to the neighboring countries of Burma (Myanmar), Sri Lanka, Thailand and others, where it had the same ennobling effect.

Five centuries after the Buddha, the noble heritage of Vipassana had disappeared from India. The purity of the teaching was lost elsewhere as well. In the country of Burma, however, it was preserved by a chain of devoted teachers. From generation to generation, for over 2000 years, this dedicated lineage transmitted the technique in its pure form.

In our time, Vipassana has been reintroduced to India, as well as to people from more than 90 other countries, by Mr. S.N. Goenka. He was authorized to teach Vipassana by the renowned Burmese Vipassana teacher, Sayagyi U Ba Khin. Before he died in 1971, U Ba Khin was able to see one of his most cherished dreams realized. He had the strong wish that Vipassana should return to India, from where, he felt sure, it would then spread throughout the world for the benefit of all mankind.

S.N. Goenka began conducting Vipassana courses in India in 1969; after ten years, he began to teach in foreign countries as well. In the decades since he started teaching, he has conducted hundreds of ten-day Vipassana courses, and trained many assistant teachers who have conducted tens of thousands of courses worldwide. In addition, more than 100 centers dedicated to the practice of Vipassana have been established: 50 in India, the remainder in 26 other countries. The invaluable gem of Vipassana, long preserved in Burma is now being practiced throughout the world. Today ever-increasing numbers of people have the opportunity to learn this art of living which brings lasting peace and happiness.

The Practice

To learn Vipassana meditation it is necessary to take a ten-day residential course under the guidance of a qualified teacher. Ten days of sustained practice have been found to be the minimum amount of time in which the essentials of the technique can be learned so that Vipassana can be applied in daily life. For the duration of the retreat, students remain within the course site, having no contact with the outside world. They refrain from reading and writing, and suspend any religious practices or other disciplines. They follow a demanding daily schedule which includes about ten hours of sitting meditation, with many breaks interspersed throughout the day. They also observe silence, not communicating with fellow students; however, they may speak with the teachers whenever necessary and they may contact the staff with needs related to food, accommodation, health and such.

There are three steps to the training. First, students practice abstaining from actions which cause harm. They undertake five moral precepts, practicing abstention from killing living beings, stealing, speaking falsely, all sexual activity and the use of intoxicants. This simple code of moral conduct, along with maintaining silence, serves to calm the mind which otherwise would be too agitated to perform the task of self observation.

The second step is to develop a more stable and concentrated mind by learning to fix one's attention on the natural reality of the ever-changing flow of the breath as it enters and leaves the nostrils. By the fourth day the mind is calmer and more focused, better able to undertake the third step, the practice of Vipassana itself: the observation of sensations throughout the body, the experiential understanding of their changing nature and the development of a balanced mind by learning not to react to them. One experiences the universal truths of impermanence, suffering and egolessness. This truth realization by direct experience is the process of purification.

The entire practice is actually a mental training. Just as physical exercises are used to improve bodily health, Vipassana can be used to develop a healthy mind.

Students receive systematic meditation instructions several times a day, and each day's progress is explained during a videotaped evening discourse by Mr. Goenka. Complete silence is observed for the first nine days. On the tenth day, students resume speaking, making the transition back to a more extroverted way of life. The course concludes on the morning of the last day.

Course Finances

All courses are run solely on a donation basis. There are no charges for the courses, not even to cover the cost of food and accommodation. All expenses are met by donations from those who, having completed a course and experienced the benefits of Vipassana, wish to give others the same opportunity. Neither the Teacher nor the assistant teachers receive remuneration; they and those who serve the courses volunteer their time. Thus Vipassana is offered free from commercialization.

A Nonsectarian Technique

Although Vipassana has been preserved in the Buddhist tradition, it contains nothing of a sectarian nature, and can be accepted and applied by people of any background. The Buddha taught Dhamma (the way, the truth, the path). The technique works on the basis that all human beings share the same problems, and that a pragmatic method which can eradicate these problems can be universally practiced. Moreover, it involves no dependence on a teacher. Vipassana teaches those who practice it to be self-dependent. Vipassana courses are open to anyone sincerely wishing to learn the technique, irrespective of race, faith or nationality. Christians, Jews, Hindus, Muslims, Buddhists and those of other religions, or no religion, have all successfully practiced Vipassana.

The malady is universal; therefore, the remedy has to be universal. For example, when we experience anger, this anger is not Christian anger or Hindu anger, Chinese anger or American anger. Similarly, love and compassion are not the strict province of any community or creed; they are universal human qualities resulting from purity of mind. People from all backgrounds who practice Vipassana find that they become better human beings.

Course Timetable

The following timetable has been designed to maintain the continuity of practice, and is used in all courses around the world.

4:00 a.m.	Wake-up bell
4:30 – 6:30 a.m.	Meditate in the meditation hall or in own room
6:30 – 8:00 a.m.	Breakfast break
8:00 – 9:00 a.m.	Group meditation in the hall
9:10 – 11:00 a.m.	Meditate in the hall or in own room as instructed
11:00 – 12 noon	Lunch break
12:00 – 1:00 p.m.	Rest; interviews with the teacher
1:00 – 2:20 p.m.	Meditate in the hall or in own room
2:30 – 3:30 p.m.	Group meditation in the hall
3:40 – 5:00 p.m.	Meditate in the hall or in own room as instructed
5:00 – 6:00 p.m.	Tea break
6:00 – 7:00 p.m.	Group meditation in the hall
7:10 – 8:15 p.m.	Teacher's discourse in the hall
8:25 – 9:00 p.m.	Group meditation in the hall
9:00 – 9:30 p.m.	Question time in the hall
9:30 p.m.	Retire; lights out

GLOSSARY

Adhiṭṭhāna	strong determination
Anattā	non-self, egoless, without essence, without substance; one of three basic characteristics along with dukkha and anicca.
Anicca	impermanence
Anapana	respiration
Anapana-sati	awareness of respiration
Bala	strength, power; the five mental strengths are faith, effort, awareness, concentration and wisdom.
Bhāvanā-maya-paññā	wisdom developing from direct personal experience
Brahma vihāra	sublime or divine state of mind in which four pure qualities are present: selfless love (mettā), compassion (karuṇā), sympathetic joy (muditā) and equanimity (upekkhā); the cultivation of these four qualities by meditation practice
Cintā-maya-paññā	wisdom gained by intellectual analysis
Dhamma	teaching of an enlightened person, the path, the way; phenomenon; object of mind; nature, natural law, truth
Dosa	aversion
Dukkha	suffering, unsatisfactoriness
Five aggregates	the basic, impermanent components of a human being: matter (rūpa), consciousness (viññāṇa), perception (saññā), sensation (vedanā) and volition (saṅkhāra)
Five hindrances	craving, aversion, mental-and-physical sluggishness, agitation, doubt
Free-world	non-incarcerated
Four causes of the arising of matter	atmosphere, nutriment, present volitional actions and past conditioned volitional actions
Four elements	water (cohesion), air (movement), fire (temperature) and earth (solidity)
Kamma (karma)	action performed by oneself that will have an effect on one's future; deep conditioning of the mind

Karuṇā	compassion
Maraṇaṃ pi dukkhaṃ	because of the arising of death, suffering arises as an effect
Mental formations	conditioned volitional actions manifesting as states and contents of mind; see saṅkhāra
Mettā	loving-kindness; selfless love
Moha	ignorance
Muditā	sympathetic joy
Namasté	traditional Indian Hindi greeting meaning "I honor the light in you."
Nibbāna	the unconditioned; the ultimate reality; freedom from suffering
Paññā	experiential wisdom developed through meditation that purifies the mind of underlying negativities
Pāramī	perfections, virtues, wholesome mental qualities that help dissolve the ego and lead one to liberation; the ten paramī are: generosity, morality, renunciation, wisdom, effort, tolerance, truthfulness, strong determination, selfless love, and equanimity
Saddha	faith, one of the five mental strengths
Samādhi	concentration; control of one's mind
Saṅkhāra	volitional activity, mental formation, reaction, mental conditioning; one of the five aggregates
Sangha	community of seekers
Sati	awareness
Sīla	morality; abstention from physical and vocal actions that cause harm to oneself and others. For a lay person sīla is practiced by following five precepts in daily life: abstaining from killing, stealing, sexual misconduct, harmful speech and intoxicants.
Storms	mental or emotional disturbances that arise during meditation
Suta-mayā-paññā	wisdom derived from listening to others; received wisdom
Sutta Nipāta	one of the collections of sayings found in the Khuddaka Nikaya of the Pāli Canon
Upekkhā	equanimity, one of the four Brahma vihārā
Viriya	effort, one of the five mental strengths; see bala

218

RESOURCES

Organizations

Vipassana Prison Trust......................................www.prison.dhamma.org

Worldwide Vipassana Centers ....www.dhamma.org

Pariyatti...www.pariyatti.org

Lionheart Foundation ....www.lionheart.org

Films

The Dhamma Brothers (2007); A Freedom Behind Bars Production, Concord, MA. Jenny Phillips, Producer; www.dhammabrothers.com. Distributor, Balcony Releasing.

Changing from Inside (1998); Donnenfield Productions, San Francisco, CA. David Donnenfield, Producer.

Doing Time, Doing Vipassana (1997); Karuna Films, Israel. Ayelet Menahemi & Eilona Ariel, Producers.

Articles and Sites

Bowen, S., Witkiewitz, K., Dillworth, T., Chawla, N., Simpson, T.L., Ostafin, B.D., Larimer, M.L., Blume, A.W. Parks, G.A. and Marlatt, G.A. "Mindfulness Meditation and Substance Use in an Incarcerated Population." *Psychology of Addictive Behaviors* 2006, Vol. 20, No. 3, 343–347.

Bowen, S., Parks, G.A., Coumar, A. & Marlatt, G.A., (2006). *Mindfulness Meditation in the Prevention and Treatment of Addictive Behaviors,* in *Buddhist Thought and Applied Psychological Research: Transcending the Boundaries,* Nauriyal, D.K., Drummond, M.S., and Lal, Y.B. (eds.) London: Routledge.

Fremon, Celeste, (2007). *America the Jailor*. Witness LA. 5 October. http://witnessla.com/prison/2007/admin/america-the-jailor/ and http://witnessla.com/category/prison-policy/

Koppel, Ted, (2007). *Breaking Point: Quick Facts*. Koppel on Discovery. 7 October. http://dsc.discovery.com/convergence/koppel/slideshows/prison-issues/prison-issues.html and http://dsc.discovery.com/convergence/koppel/highlights/highlights.html

Macaillar, Daniel, (1996). *From Classroom to Cell Blocks: How Prison Building Affects Higher Education and African American Enrollment in California.* Center on Juvenile and Criminal Justice, 2002. http://www.cjcj.org/pubs/higher/highercal.html

Marlatt, G.A., et al., (2004). *Vipassana Meditation as a Treatment for Alcohol and Drug Use Disorders,* in *Mindfulness and Acceptance: Expanding the Cognitive-Behavioral Tradition,* S.C. Hayes, V.M. Follete, and M.M. Linehan (eds.) New York: Guilford Press.

Meijer, L., (1999). "Vipassana Meditation at the North Rehabilitation Facility." *American Jails Magazine,* July/August.

Parks, G.A., Marlatt, G.A., et al., (2003). "The University of Washington Vipassana Meditation Research Project at the North Rehabilitation Facility." *American Jails Magazine,* July/August.

ABOUT THE AUTHOR

Jenny Phillips has a doctorate in cultural anthropology and is a practicing psychotherapist in her hometown of Concord, Massachusetts. She also works in state and county prisons, teaching courses on emotional literacy skills. Her articles have appeared in academic journals, *The Boston Globe*, and national magazines.

The author with two of the Dhamma Brothers at Donaldson

She first visited Donaldson Prison in 1999, where her initiative led to the establishment of a Vipassana program. Since then Jenny has received more than 200 letters from the inmates documenting their lives in prison and their quest for inner peace. She also produced and directed *The Dhamma Brothers*, an award-winning documentary film about this program and its participants at Donaldson, which was released in 2008.

In 2002 Jenny founded The Hemingway Preservation Foundation to support the work of the Cuban government in preserving the Cuban home, library and papers of Ernest Hemingway. Jenny's grandfather, Maxwell Perkins, was Hemingway's editor and close friend. With her husband Frank Phillips, State House bureau chief for *The Boston Globe*, she has traveled extensively throughout Cuba researching and collecting oral history and artifacts about Hemingway's 22 years there.

PRAISE FOR *LETTERS FROM THE DHAMMA BROTHERS*

"In the Civil Rights Movement, we used the wisdom of India and Mohandas Gandhi, to create a discipline and philosophy of nonviolence that would meet the needs of the American landscape. The Dhamma Brothers have taken their own passage to India and discovered a practice of meditation that guides them down their inner path toward freedom. Those of us who accept the philosophy of nonviolence believe there is a spark of divinity within all of us. This book makes it plain that no human being—no matter how troubled his beginning, regardless of his race, color, nationality, or creed—should be considered beyond the reach of redemption. No one should be tossed away in a jail cell and forgotten as though his life means nothing. This book demonstrates that all some people need—even those we might consider the worst among us—is to be led toward their path to recovery, and when they are restored, their contribution to our society and the world is limitless."

—U.S. Congressman John Lewis, civil rights leader and author, Walking with the Wind: A Memoir of the Movement

"This is an absolutely compelling story of an astonishing treatment program with prison inmates that, against all odds, actually worked. The magic combination of Jenny Phillips, the leaders of the program and the correctional officials opened a door to the hearts and minds of a violent prison population, allowing us to see them at intimate range, while at the same time producing a remarkably positive influence on the atmosphere of the prison as a whole. It is a book that should reshape the ideas of all of us—policymakers and citizens alike."

—Doris Kearns Goodwin, Pulitzer Prize author, presidential historian; author, Team of Rivals: The Political Genius of Abraham Lincoln

"The stories of the Dhamma Brothers ring with the truth and power of their experiences, and offer the hope for renewal and rehabilitation within a dismal and punishment-oriented correctional system. It gives one hope in the human race."

—Sister Helen Prejean, author, Dead Man Walking *and Recipient, 1996 Pax Christi Pope Paul VI Teacher of Peace Award*

"This is a radical book in the true sense of the word radical—going to the root. [It] shows how maximum-security prisoners transformed themselves and their relationships with others through the practice of Vipassana meditation. In letters and interviews, the prisoners describe what it is like going to the root of their own abusive, addictive habit patterns, deeply entrenched since childhood, and what changes came as a result: in short, how they became more patient, more loving, more peaceful, even in the face of overwhelming violence. The prisoners' struggles, setbacks, and astounding successes will inspire the free world reader or any reader to greater efforts at self-knowledge and self-understanding."

—*Rebecca Lemov, author,* World as Laboratory: Experiments with Mice, Mazes, and Men; *Assistant Visiting Professor, Harvard University*

"This book is one of the most sensitive expressions of hope, capacity for change and potential vehicles for institutional health that I have read in my career in criminal justice. Inmates serving long sentences in one of the country's toughest state prisons discuss the liberating effect of the Vipassana meditation program. The writers provide a dramatic example of a safe and healthy correctional environment, not only for the inmates but also for the correction officers and all the people who must work within these institutions, and points to an effective reentry program for even the most serious offenders in our society.

Phillips has added a major piece of literature to the correctional library that should be read by every correctional administrator and public policy leader. If these program results can be replicated—given the minimal investment and the maximum potential of the results—the human, social and economic costs of incarceration could be dramatically mitigated for all of us, not just the inmates.

The book directly addresses the potential for cynicism and skepticism by the reader: as we learn about these individuals, we realize that they are accepting responsibility for their serious crimes, attempting to engage in personal change even though it will not enable them to be released but allow them to serve out their time and life in a more positive way."

—*Scott Harshbarger, former Attorney General of Massachusetts; past chair of a correctional reform commission, Massachusetts*

"A must-read for anyone interested in contemplative practices in correctional settings, and professionals interested in alternative programs and interventions."

—*Dave Murphy, Program Manager, Department of Community & Human Services; former administrator, North Rehabilitation Facility, Seattle*

"An inspiring account, largely through their own words, of personal transformation through meditation in inmates at a maximum security prison. This is a must-read for policymakers and penal administrators and it will inspire all by the compelling stories of personal growth in the harshest of conditions."

—*Richard Davidson, Director, Wisconsin Center for Affective Science, and Center for Mind-Body Interaction, University of Wisconsin-Madison*

"I highly recommend this book for readers who are looking for signs of awakening…behind prison walls. Each interview and letter tells a unique story, often filled with visions of hope and compassion in an otherwise desperate situation. Thanks to Jenny Phillips for bringing this to light."

—*Alan Marlatt, Professor and Director, Addictive Behaviors Research Center, University of Washington Dept. of Psychology*

ABOUT PARIYATTI

Pariyatti is dedicated to providing affordable access to authentic teachings from the Buddha about the Dhamma theory (*pariyatti*) and practice (*paṭipatti*) of Vipassana meditation. A 501(c)(3) nonprofit charitable organization since 2002, Pariyatti is sustained by contributions from individuals who appreciate and want to share the incalculable value of the Dhamma teachings. We invite you to visit www.pariyatti.org to learn about our programs, services, and ways to support publishing and other undertakings.

Pariyatti Publishing imprints

Vipassana Research Publications (focus on Vipassana as taught by S.N. Goenka in the tradition of Sayagyi U Ba Khin)

BPS Pariyatti Editions (selected titles from the Buddhist Publication Society, copublished by Pariyatti in the Americas)

Pariyatti Digital Editions (audio and video titles, including discourses)

Pariyatti Press (inspirational writing by contemporary meditators)

Selected works published by Pariyatti

Discourse Summaries, by S.N. Goenka

Karma and Chaos, by Paul R. Fleischman, MD

Meditation Now, by S.N. Goenka

A Comprehensive Manual of Abhidhamma, Bhikkhu Bodhi, ed.

The Life of the Buddha, by Ven. Ñanamoli

Cultivating Inner Peace, by Paul R. Fleischman, MD

The Moon Appears When the Water is Still, by Ian McCrorie

Pariyatti
867 Larmon Road, Onalaska, WA 98570, USA
Tel. 360.978.4998
www.pariyatti.org | publisher@pariyatti.org

Letters from the Dhamma Brothers is distributed to the trade by Independent Publishers Group
For information about the film, *The Dhamma Brothers,* visit www.dhammabrothers.com